"To read this book is to learn from women in the Bible who've experienced the presence of God. Joanna Harader extends to us their companionship during our journey through Lent—to open ourselves to their instruction, their faith, as we wander through the wilderness of this world. With them we await the God who provides—the One who nurtures the gift of hope amid abandonment, who promises life despite our violence. These pages will renew your capacity to recognize the signs and wonders of God's provision, sometimes as close as the hand of a friend or the generosity of a stranger."

—**ISAAC VILLEGAS**, author of *Migrant God: A Christian Vision for Immigrant Justice*

"Joanna Harader invites us on a rich and thoughtful sojourn through Lent alongside women who braved the wilderness but also reached out to the vulnerable, stood up to the powerful, listened to their love and desire, followed Jesus to his death, and then proclaimed his resurrection. Along the way, we encounter such powerful images, soul-stirring words, and excellent questions—this book will deepen Lent for all its readers!"

—**HEIDI HAVERKAMP**, spiritual director, Episcopal priest, and author or editor of several books, including *Everyday Connections: Reflections and Practices for Year B*

"In *Prone to Wander*, Joanna Harader invites us to journey in and through the wilderness of Lent, introducing us to the women of the Bible as we go. Through familiar and not-so-familiar stories, we ponder themes of power and authority, love and grace, faithfulness and salvation. With her gentle encouragement and probing questions, Harader proves to be a wise and steady companion along the way."

—**LEE HULL MOSES**, author of *More Than Enough: Living Abundantly in a Culture of Excess*

D1520681

"Like Mary at Jesus' feet, I found myself in a state of teary-eyed, peaceful reverence while reading this devotional. *Prone to Wander* feels like a refreshing journey and a warm meal all at the same time. In honoring the stories of often-overlooked women in Scripture, Joanna Harader helps us listen closely to God and reminds us that our story, too, matters to God. You don't need to polish yourself up for this kind of Bible study. Show up as you are and find gentle, true nourishment."

—**CARISSA CAPLES**, content writer at Honeycomb Media

PRONE to WANDER

PRONE to WANDER

A LENTEN JOURNEY with WOMEN
in the WILDERNESS

JOANNA HARADER

Original artwork by
MICHELLE BURKHOLDER

HERALD
P R E S S

Harrisonburg, Virginia

To my dear spiritual encouragers and faithful wilderness companions:
cohort two (aka "the best cohort") and my morning prayer group.
With deep and abiding gratitude.
—Joanna Harader

For Becky and Simon, with gratitude for all the ways you wander,
wonder, and vista hunt with me.
—Michelle Burkholder

Herald Press
PO Box 866, Harrisonburg, Virginia 22803
www.HeraldPress.com

Library of Congress cataloging-in-publication data has been applied for.

Study guides are available for many Herald Press titles at www.HeraldPress.com.

PRONE TO WANDER
© 2025 by Joanna Haradar, Harrisonburg, Virginia 22803. 800-245-7894.
    All rights reserved.
Library of Congress Control Number: 2024033453
International Standard Book Number: 978-1-5138-1481-0 (paperback);
    978-1-5138-1482-7 (ebook)
Cover and interior design by Merrill Miller. Cover illustration adapted from Getty Images.
Printed in United States of America

Original artwork on pages 12, 34, 56, 78, 100, 122, 144, 160, and 182 by Michelle Burkholder.
Author photo by Kelsey Kimberlina.

29 28 27 26 25   10 9 8 7 6 5 4 3 2 1

CONTENTS

AN INVITATION FROM
THE AUTHOR

As we enter this season of Lent, I invite you to come and wander with me in the wilderness. We will keep company with biblical women who live in the literal wild spaces of desert and forest, those who inhabit landscapes of travel and exile, and those who dwell in the figurative wilderness of fear, pain, and grief. While their physical landscapes may be unfamiliar, I expect you will recognize the emotional landscapes quite well.

So I invite you into the familiar unknown. I invite you into the paradox of the wilderness.

This is a place of deprivation and of deep provision. In this barren landscape where water and food can be hard to come by, our spirits feel brittle, daily life seems a struggle, and loneliness threatens to overwhelm us. But sometimes manna appears like dew glistening in the sun. We don't know what it is or where it came from, but it sustains us along the way. Sometimes we come across a flowing stream, a hidden well, a mysterious source of refreshing water, welcome and unexpected.

This is a place where we face disorientation and where we find clarity. It can be difficult to discern our way in the wilderness because everything looks the same no matter which way we turn. When all paths lead through the same terrain, it's impossible to tell where they might end, which makes it almost impossible to know how to start. This disorientation is an invitation to pause, to breathe, to rest. If we cannot find our way, perhaps the way will find us.

The wilderness is both a dangerous space and a sacred space. Hunger and thirst, heat and cold, wild animals and treacherous terrain all threaten our health, our safety, even our lives. Yet these very conditions can bring us face-to-face with God—which is, I suppose, its own kind of danger. For so many of these biblical women, the wilderness is sacred space. It is the threatening and holy space where they encounter their full selves and the fullness of the Holy One.

To willingly enter the wilderness of Lent is an unfathomable act for those who prioritize ease and comfort. But these women in the wilderness remind us that deprivation can allow for deep provision, that disorientation is a precursor to clarity. If we want to live fully, we have to live bravely. If we hope to meet God, we have to venture into the frightening and sacred places where God so often shows up. Or rather, places where we are more likely to take notice of God's presence. Because in these wilderness places, our illusions of self-sufficiency are wiped away and we are forced to cry out to God, who will hear and answer, who will provide for our needs and accompany us on the path.

So welcome to the wilderness, friends. I am so glad you have chosen to join me on this journey.

SUGGESTIONS FOR USING THIS DEVOTIONAL

The daily devotions in this book begin with Ash Wednesday and continue through the first week of the Easter season to the Sunday after Easter. The Sunday readings provide blessings in the voices of biblical women. All other daily readings include a scripture reference, a reflection on the passage, a suggested spiritual practice, and questions to consider.

The spiritual practices identified in the "Connect" section for each day invite you into a wide range of activities designed to help you connect more deeply with God, yourself, and other people. While you are certainly welcome to engage with all the "Connect" prompts, they are in no way intended to be assignments for you to fulfill. Perhaps there are certain days you have extra time to do the suggested practice, or maybe you want to choose one each week to explore. If you find a practice—from this book or elsewhere—that is particularly meaningful in this season, you are welcome to return to that practice repeatedly and see how it interacts with the stories that we will explore together.

You might want to address the "Consider" questions in a formal manner through journaling or simply think about them, holding them lightly throughout your day. These questions may prove especially fruitful for discussions around the dinner table or in small groups. Most of the questions are more personal than biblical and can therefore be used with groups that include those unfamiliar with the specific stories addressed in the reflections.

A significant aspect of this devotional is the artwork provided by my dear friend and colleague, Rev. Michelle Burkholder. Michelle has designed an image to accompany each blessing, along with a labyrinth image you will find on page 12 of this book. These images invite you into prayerful consideration and wandering as you move through this season of Lent. The "Connect" activity for Wednesday during week 2 of Lent (p. 46) specifically directs you to the labyrinth image. You may choose to use the labyrinth frequently, perhaps as a way to center yourself in preparation for reading or as you contemplate the "Consider" questions after a reflection.

Finally, in addition to using this book for personal prayer and reflection, you might also like to explore these stories with a group. At the back of the book, you will find some resources for using this material in worship, with small groups, and on retreats. However you engage with *Prone to Wander*, I pray that these biblical women will prove faithful guides for your own wilderness wandering this Lenten season.

A NOTE FROM THE ARTIST

The process of collaborating with Joanna on her first book, *Expecting Emmanuel*, was full of surprises, challenge, and joy. I expected no less from the journey as we set out to create *Prone to Wander*, and I was not disappointed. Designing and crafting paper cutouts in response to Joanna's writing is a unique experience. Joanna's words are full of rich imagery and emotion on their own; what can visual reflections offer to them? In the case of the blessings and images found within these pages, I experience them as an exploration of a wilderness journey into the season of Lent through the invitation of Joanna's writings.

The series of images created for this volume are naturescapes—small wilderness vistas into imaginary landscapes that play with the themes and words of the blessings they accompany. In many of the pieces, the reader encounters a literal pathway traversing the page. In some cases, the path is obstructed, and in others it may be hard to distinguish the paths from other elements in the image.

The images are a visual reflection on the various natures of wilderness itself. Sometimes it is clear that we are on a wilderness path. Other times our wilderness experiences are challenging to navigate, and we have less clarity on how we will journey through the moment at hand. In a few of the pieces, the path is not visibly present at all. These are a reminder of the wilderness spaces that invite, or sometimes force, us to be present with what is, whether beautiful or messy. The path in these moments of wilderness is not through or to somewhere else—it is instead a journey inward. Joanna's words and the season of Lent invite us to journey into a variety of wilderness spaces and encourage us to be transformed by them.

The pieces of art found in these pages are all paper cutouts, single sheets of paper transformed into images through hand-cut lines and shapes. As the cut pieces are removed, the resulting image reveals itself. In a time when crisp digital and AI imagery is so prevalent, the imperfect and wobbly lines of these cutouts are a reminder and celebration of the complex wilderness of being human. May the resulting images be a space of visual rest, challenge, exploration, and invitation to accompany you on your own wilderness journey.

—*Michelle Burkholder*

AT HOME

—

Welcome to the Wilderness

ASH WEDNESDAY

READ

Exodus 13:17–22

REFLECT

On this Ash Wednesday, perhaps you will receive (or already have received) the imposition of ashes: "From dust you have come, and to dust you shall return." Each year, as I draw the sooty cross on offered foreheads, my practice is to add, "God is with you on the journey." I do not speak these words simply to ease the doom and gloom of traditional Ash Wednesday observances. I speak them because the experiences of my life and the witness of Scripture affirm the truth of God's presence with God's people even in the most difficult times.

The people of the exodus bear witness to dramatic examples of God's presence in the wilderness. And so these desert wanderers seem to be especially helpful companions as we enter the season of Lent. While today's scripture passage does not mention any particular women, you can be sure there were plenty of women among these people whom God is leading: mothers with infants strapped to their bodies, stopping to nurse along the way; grandmothers being pushed in carts by a rotating crew of children and grandchildren; bossy big sisters keeping their younger siblings in line; young women singing and laughing and braiding each other's hair.

When we are in our own places of fear and uncertainty, it is worth noting how God leads these women (and the others who accompany them). First, we learn that "God did not lead them by way of the land of the Philistines . . . [but] by the roundabout way of the wilderness" (vv. 17–18). The "way of the Philistines," also known as the Via Maris, was a prominent ancient trade route. It would have been a relatively direct and smooth route; but it also would have been more dangerous than the path they took. Isn't that so often the case? The shortest route is not always the best or most faithful. The route we prefer, the one that avoids the wilderness, may hold dangers we can't see, whereas the roundabout way may provide blessings we cannot anticipate.

God leads the people "by a roundabout way" in order to avoid war with the Philistines, yet the people are still "prepared for battle" (v. 18). I recoil a bit at this military language, but when taken as a metaphor, I appreciate the general sentiment that we should enter the wilderness prepared. Because if there is one thing we can expect in the wilderness, it is the unexpected: mysterious food, water from a rock, thundering clouds, rampant serpents. It is wise to enter new situations with all that God provides; it is wise to be "prepared for battle" even if we don't think there will be any battles to fight. Whenever you start something new—when you embark on a course of study, commit to a partner, become a parent, join a church, accept a job offer—you may think you know what you are signing up for, but chances are you actually have no idea. You'll need to be prepared for whatever the wilderness brings, not just for what you expect to encounter.

Another notable, if odd, detail in today's passage is that Moses brings along the bones of Joseph. Even though the people are fleeing slavery in Egypt, they do not leave the entirety of their past behind. Carrying Joseph's bones (and eventually those of Moses) is a way to honor the ancestors. It is also a way to carry the stories of those who have navigated the wilderness before them, stories of how God has been present with their people in the past. When all seems hopeless, these bones can bring hope. When the people feel irretrievably lost, these bones can provide a way forward. The bones may be a bit cumbersome, but they are also necessary.

Finally, we have what is perhaps the most dramatic and enviable feature of the wilderness journey: a pillar of cloud by day and a pillar of fire by night. I have longed for such clear signs of God's leading, especially in the wilderness where the landscape looks the same all the way around. It's sand or trees or rocks or manicured lawns as far as the eye can see. How can we know which direction to go? Pillars of cloud and fire would, indeed, provide welcome clarity. But I have found that in my own wilderness places, God's leading tends to be more nuanced and subtle. We may not have the benefit of flaming and glowing pillars along our own paths, yet we can still cling to the promise of God's presence. We can look to the women of the exodus and be assured of God's faithful guidance.

Welcome to the wilderness. From dust we have come; to dust we shall return. And God, indeed, is with us on this journey.

CONNECT

Consider what "bones" you want to carry with you into the Lenten wilderness. What stories from the past—of your familial ancestors, predecessors in the faith, or others—can provide you with hope, inspiration, and grounding in this season? Find a box in which you can place reminders of these stories. You might write names on slips of paper (perhaps shaped like bones) or find pictures or other items that bring to mind the people and stories you want to carry with you.

CONSIDER

When in your life has God led you by a roundabout way? Looking back, can you see some benefit in taking a longer, more difficult route than was strictly necessary? Assuming that God does not appear to you as pillars of cloud and fire, how *do* you experience God's leading in your life? What signs do you look for?

FOUNT OF EVERY BLESSING
—
Eve Who Mothers All

THURSDAY
EVE BECOMES

READ

Genesis 2:15–25

REFLECT

If we think of wilderness as a completely unfamiliar and disorienting place, then these first humans are in the wildest wilderness anyone has ever experienced. Literally every single thing they encounter is brand new—not just to them in particular, but to humanity in general. They themselves are brand new, even their own bodies a deep mystery.

The Hebrew word translated in Genesis as "man" *before* the woman is created is a different word than that translated as "man" *after* the woman is created. The first term, *adam*, can be read as gender-neutral: the human.[1] So I invite you to consider this first human as many-gendered. The person whom God forms from the dust and breathes life into (Genesis 2:7) encompasses the fullness of humanity. As the first human carries no particular gender identity, they therefore carry all genders. And so we see that women have been in the wilderness since creation.

Going back to the beginning, then, seems like a good place to start our journey. While this story from Genesis 2 is the second creation story we encounter in Scripture, it was likely the first of the two biblical creation stories to circulate within the oral tradition of the Jewish people. In this story we learn that, from the beginning, God has helped humans navigate even the most disorienting of wilderness spaces.

First, God puts the human in the garden to "till it and keep it" (v. 15). The human might not know where they are or how everything works or what is happening, but they find themselves in a specific place with a specific task. However chaotic life is, this seems a good starting point: Where am I right now? What good thing is in front of me to do?

God also provides for the human's physical needs with an abundance of food growing on the trees. Provision in the wilderness is a story told over and over again in Scripture: from the first human in Eden to the Israelites in the desert to Jesus feeding the multitudes on the hillside. The wilderness is less scary if we trust that God will provide for our needs while we are there.

Then, of course, there is God's questionable prohibition of eating from the tree of knowledge of good and evil. It seems like a rather cruel and arbitrary thing to stick a beautiful tree right there in the middle of the garden and tell the human they can't eat the fruit. Excessive amounts of theological ink have been spilled over this passage, and I'm not in a position to give a comprehensive explanation of God's reasoning on this (or anything else). But I do invite you to consider what God's command here might suggest about how we can navigate our own wilderness. Perhaps it shows that boundaries can be helpful; sometimes rules and guidelines are freeing rather than oppressive. Part of the problem in the wilderness is that there are too many options: too much space, too many directions to choose from. If we can rule out even one of the options, it can help us choose a path and start making our way. Sometimes boundaries and limits are not arbitrary, nor are they punishments—rather, they are helpful guides on the journey.

When God invites the human to name all the animals, it is a way for the human to exercise some control over a situation that surely feels completely out of control. The human may not understand how that creature flies, but they can call it a bird; that furry creature with spots that runs impossibly fast may still be a mystery, but at least they can name it 'cheetah'. In the wilderness, even claiming small amounts of power—like linguistic power—can help us cope with the feeling of powerlessness that we so often experience.

Of course, God and the human realize that even with the abundant food, the helpful boundaries, the naming of animals, something is still missing, something the human needs to be able to thrive in the wilderness.

It turns out that this missing piece is human companionship: "bone of my bones and flesh of my flesh" (v. 23). The human, *adam*, becomes woman (*isshah*) and man (*ish*). The one becomes two and will soon become many.

This, it turns out, is what we most need to navigate the wilderness: each other. It did not work—it never works—for one person to hold all the pieces of identity and skill and power within oneself. We each hold only some of the pieces; we need one another as partners to make our way in the wilderness.

And so, my friends, I invite you to gather what you need for this wilderness journey. Be present where you are. Tend to the tasks that are before you. Honor the boundaries and limits of your life for now. Trust in God's provision. Exercise your power. And find the other humans with whom you can partner on this journey.

CONNECT

Spend some time outside observing wild creatures: birds, bugs, any fun, furry critters you might see. Notice how they navigate the wilderness: Where do they get food? How do they find shelter? How do they relate to other animals? Offer a prayer of thanks for God's good creation in the place you inhabit.

CONSIDER

Reread the final paragraph of today's reflection. Choose one of the invitations that you find most challenging, and consider how you can move toward accepting that invitation in this season of Lent.

FRIDAY
EVE DECIDES

READ

Genesis 3:1–7

REFLECT

Even though the garden of Eden is allegedly paradise, it is also wilderness. The human ones inhabit a newly created place in new bodies as they navigate new relationships with creation and with each other. Every sight, sound, taste, smell, and texture must have been delightful and disorienting all at once.

The one grounding reality amid the wilderness was the Creator—the God who formed and loved and was present with the human ones as they navigated this unfamiliar landscape. Then the crafty serpent slithered up to Eve and threw her into a theological wilderness with one question: "Did God say . . . ?" (v. 1). The serpent, of course, is making it up. God definitely didn't say that the humans could not eat from any tree in the garden, and the woman tells him so. But even as the woman explains what God did *not* say, she begins to question what God *did* say.

Magicians sometimes use a technique called "pushing a card." They tell a random audience member to "pick any card," but then subtly feed them a particular one. The person thinks they have free choice, but they are actually taking the card the magician wants them to take. The serpent is crafty; he's a good magician, an expert, it seems, at pushing cards. He makes an incorrect statement so that Eve can correct him and feel like the authority in the situation. He draws the woman's attention to the one forbidden tree that she had not been concerned about before. And so Eve's decision is not entirely her decision, even though it feels like her own free choice.

At the beginning of their conversation, Eve is clear about what God has said and seems committed to following God's instructions—because she trusts God's good intentions. The serpent subtly whittles away at Eve's trust in God, calling into question not only the accuracy of God's statements but also the intent and character of God. Eve goes from resting in the care and guidance of her loving Creator to believing she has to figure things out for herself—that she is responsible for knowing good from evil, for covering her nakedness.

I have to be honest with you here and admit to my own wilderness wandering when it comes to this foundational faith story. I resonate with the woman's questioning, her wondering, her desire to make her own decisions and try to more deeply understand this new world she is inhabiting. I am not a fan of obedience for the sake of obedience, even when it is obedience to God.

No. That's not it. I fully support obedience to God. I just don't think we can ever be certain about what is true obedience to God and what is merely obedience to people who are trying to convince us they speak for God. The serpents are still pushing cards quite skillfully.

"Did God really say . . . ?"

It is a good question for the wilderness. A question we shouldn't be afraid to ask. A question we should earnestly try to answer. The wilderness is a place where much is unclear, which makes it very tempting to reach for any type of certainty we can find. But when we try to escape the wilderness of questions with hasty answers, we often sacrifice divine truth for the sake of perceived clarity.

With Eve's story in mind, I encourage you to let yourself wander in the wilderness this Lent. Sit with the questions, however uncomfortable. And beware the serpents who so skillfully push you to doubt the goodness of your Creator.

CONNECT

Eat a piece of your favorite fruit. Give thanks to God for delightful abundance.

CONSIDER

Fill in the blank with what you have been told God said but aren't quite sure about: Did God really say _____? Spend some time considering, journaling about, discussing, or researching this question.

SATURDAY
EVE CAST OUT

READ

Genesis 3:8–24

REFLECT

"They heard the sound of the LORD God walking in the garden at the time of the evening breeze" (v. 8).

It sounds lovely, doesn't it? Strolling through the garden as the air begins to cool and a soft breeze rustles the leaves of the beautiful trees. God by your side in this spectacular new world. It sounds like paradise. But the man and woman are not happy to hear God's footfall. They do not want to walk beside God in the quiet of the evening. They want God to leave them alone, so they hide among the trees.

We theoretically long for God's presence in the wilderness, but in reality the divine footfall is often an unwelcome sound. Like Eve, we realize that God's presence means accountability. It means facing the consequences of decisions we have made. It means answering uncomfortable questions.

Questions like, "Where are you?" (v. 9). The text says God called to the man, but this is clearly a question for both of the human ones: Where are you? I've long been perplexed by this question. God surely knew where the people were—they had just scampered off to crouch behind a tree. It's a comical scene really, like when a little kid pulls a blanket over their head thinking Mom won't know where they went.

So maybe God, ever the gracious mother, is just playing along with her children's ridiculous game of hide-and-seek. "Oh no, wherever did those silly people go?" Or maybe God is asking the question that the humans need to ask of themselves: Where are we?

Aside from the simple and unnecessary response—"Here, behind a tree!"—how might the human ones answer this question? Where are they, indeed. And *where am I?* Where is this place that I stand in relation to the vastness that God has created? Who is this person that I am in relation to all the other creations of God? How does my newly emerging understanding and knowledge affect how I relate to other creatures and to the Holy One, my Creator?

Where am I?

That's the question of the wilderness, a question for us to carry in this Lenten season and beyond.

It becomes obvious from Eve's encounter with God in the garden that even when we cannot answer the question for ourselves, God knows where we are—for better, which sometimes feels like for worse. I can imagine Eve praying the words of Psalm 139:

> Where can I go from your spirit?
>   Or where can I flee from your presence? . . .
> How weighty to me are your thoughts, O God!
>   How vast is the sum of them!
> I try to count them—they are more than the sand;
>   I come to the end—I am still with you. (vv. 7, 17–18)

"I am still with you." You are still with me. Wherever Eve is, she is with God. Wherever we are, God is there. Even as we try to hide.

There are so many uncomfortable questions in the wilderness. Questions like, "What have you done?" Just as God knew where the humans were, God also knew what they had done. God does not ask this question to obtain information, but to give the woman an opportunity to enter into conversation with God about her choices and their consequences. The woman, however, does not use this as a chance for self-reflection but rather blames the serpent for what she has done. The blame is not altogether misplaced, but it is also not helpful for her personal growth or her relationship with God.

The serpent, the woman, and the man all face consequences for their actions. These consequences are often understood as punishment from God, but we can also understand them as God simply explaining what the results of their actions will be. In this new world where all the relationships are getting figured out, the consequences of the humans' choices are relational.

The relationship between people and other creatures is disrupted: there is enmity between the serpent and humans. The relationships of humans with one another are disrupted: the man will rule over the woman; this is not the ideal, not the way relationships are supposed to work. And the relationship of humans to the land is disrupted: people will toil to bring food from the land. The ancient people who told this story around the campfire and those who finally wrote it down surely recognized the brokenness of these relationships in their own world, just as we can recognize the brokenness in ours.

This story is one attempt to answer another uncomfortable question: Why? Why aren't things perfect? Why do we struggle with each other and our environment and God?

Despite all the uncomfortable questions and the hard truths in this passage, we end on a note of grace. We end with God making garments for the human ones. These are garments that God knows they don't need; garments that God wishes they didn't want. And still God sews clothes for them. Which may be the most tender gesture of grace in all of Scripture.

The wilderness, my friends, is full of questions. I pray you have the courage to come out of hiding and answer them honestly. I pray you can trust in the grace of your Creator as you make your way through this uncharted territory.

CONNECT

On this Lenten journey, we want to come out of hiding and allow ourselves to be fully known by God. Read Psalm 139. Choose a quote from the psalm to write on a sticky note and put it where you can be reminded of God's presence with you each day.

CONSIDER

Ponder one or more of the wilderness questions from this passage:

Where are you?
What have you done?
Why?

Blessing for the First Sunday of Lent: Eve's Blessing

Welcome to the wilderness, beloveds.
Look at the lush landscape.
Listen for the birds, the brook's babble, the song of wind in the trees.
Feel the breeze.
Smell the earth,
Taste everything you can—
    let the sweet and bitter dance on your tongue.

Welcome to the wilderness, beloveds,
where you may soon realize
that the lushness disorients;
that though you can hear the brook, you cannot find it to get a drink;
that the breeze carries bits of grit that sting your face
and scents that make you cover your nose.

Welcome to the wilderness,
where all that seems good to eat is not,
but some of it is,
and it's oh so hard to tell the difference.

Since I have been here for a while
    (the longest while),
allow me to offer a few words as gift and guide:
    breathe in the beauty;
    love the questions
        and be brave in the asking and answering;
    do not be ashamed.
Trust that God's presence is grace.
Always grace.
Amen.

WEEK 2

STREAMS OF MERCY
—
Hagar Who Names God

MONDAY
HAGAR ENSLAVED

READ

Genesis 16:1–6

REFLECT

The text says that Sarai "gave [Hagar] to her husband Abram as a wife" (v. 3), but Hagar was not Abram's wife in the way we understand marriage today. As an enslaved person, Hagar has no agency or consent in this situation, and therefore when Abram impregnates Hagar, that is an act of rape. Sarai treats Hagar's body as property to be used for Sarai's purposes: if Sarai wants a drink, Hagar brings it to her; if Sarai wants food, Hagar makes it; if Sarai wants her clothes clean, Hagar washes them; if Sarai wants a baby, Hagar gets impregnated, carries the child, and gives birth.

Is it any wonder that Hagar looks at Sarai "with contempt" (v. 5)? In Sarai's mind, Hagar looks down on her because Hagar has become pregnant while Sarai has not been able to conceive. But this understanding of Hagar's "contempt" probably has a lot more to do with Sarai than with Hagar. Sarai clearly feels inferior because of her childless status. She feels ashamed of what her body has not done and considers herself less than women who have borne children. Sarai may have sincere personal desires for a child of her own; she also lives in a culture that ties women's value to their ability to bear children. If Sarai cannot have children, she cannot give her husband an all-important heir. She is not viewed as worthwhile or productive, and people will start to wonder why God is punishing her.

In reality, I imagine that Hagar's contempt is not about her feeling superior, but about her resenting this situation that Sarai and Abram have put her in. Hagar is enslaved and sexually exploited, which results in her pregnancy. While Sarai longs for a child, an heir, we cannot assume Hagar has the same desire. As someone enslaved, any children she bore would also be enslaved, and there was no guarantee she would even get to keep them and raise them. Pregnancy is physically exhausting, and in Hagar's day it carried significant risk of maternal death. Hagar has many reasons to avoid pregnancy.

In this story, Abram reminds me of the man in Eve's story: he does something that his partner tells him to do and then does not want to take any responsibility for his actions. When Sarai complains to him about Hagar's "contempt," Abram could have talked through the situation with her, or he could have offered to deal with Hagar (since he impregnated her). But instead he says, "Your slave is in your power." The person with the greatest power in the system abdicates that power when it becomes inconvenient.

And so, with nobody to challenge Sarai's perspective or step in on Hagar's behalf, Sarai takes matters into her own hands. She "dealt harshly with" Hagar (v. 6). Again the text seems to gloss over the violence done to Hagar. We do not know exactly what Sarai does, but whatever form the abuse takes, it is significant enough that Hagar runs away.

She runs *to* the wilderness. Because for Hagar, the wilderness seems like a better option than enslavement. The exposure to the elements, the thirst and potential starvation—it all seems preferable to the treatment she faces as Sarai's slave. In her desperation, the pregnant Hagar flees to the wilderness, seeking safety for herself and her child.

The wilderness, it seems, is not always a place of despair. It can be a place of freedom from the confines and abuses of "civilized" society. Sometimes we *choose* the wilderness as a place of respite and refuge.

CONNECT

Offer prayers for—and perhaps some money to—an organization in your community that supports people who are trying to escape the wilderness of violent situations.

CONSIDER

Sarai becomes upset by what she imagines Hagar is thinking about her. Do you ever do this? Is there someone whom you imagine is upset or angry or disappointed with you right now? Is it possible that what you imagine isn't actually what they are feeling? How can you have compassion for that person and for yourself as you navigate the relationship?

TUESDAY
HAGAR NAMES GOD

READ

Genesis 16:7–16

REFLECT

This scene of Hagar in the wilderness reminds me of the scene with Eve in Eden. God comes looking for her and then asks a significant question. In Eve's case, God asks, "Where are you?" (Genesis 3:9). For Hagar, God sends a messenger, who does not question where she is now, but wants to know, "Where have you come from and where are you going?" Hagar responds: "I am running away from my mistress Sarai" (16:8). This seems to answer the first part of the question—she has come from Sarai's household. But it does not indicate where Hagar is going. "Away" is not a clear destination.

On one level, I find the angel's instruction for Hagar to return and submit to Sarai to be quite problematic. God is sending Hagar back to her abusers, back to a place from which she has been desperate to leave. Still, as we know from contemporary reality, abusive situations are difficult to escape, and running away is not always the best or safest course of action. As a young, pregnant woman with (as far as we know) no community or family ties outside of Sarai's household, it is difficult to imagine how Hagar would survive—and keep her child alive—in the wilderness.

As much as Hagar does not want to go back, and as much as we might not want her to go back, and regardless of whether returning is, in fact, her best possibility for survival, Hagar leaves the wilderness and returns to Sarai's household. But the angel does not send her without hope. The promise that God makes to Hagar echoes the promise that God has made to Abram. In Genesis 15:5, God says to Abram: "Look toward heaven and count the stars . . . so shall your descendants be." Here, God makes Hagar a similar, and possibly even grander, promise: "I will so greatly multiply your offspring that they cannot be counted for multitude" (16:10).

In that cultural context, children were the ultimate blessing, so this is truly an astonishing promise for God to make to an enslaved Egyptian woman. The rest of the blessing, though, seems a bit strange: that Ishmael will be a "wild ass of a man," and "he shall live at odds with all his kin" (v. 12). This is not the blessing I would hope to receive about my child, but perhaps Hagar hears it differently than I do. As an enslaved person, she can expect that her child will also be enslaved. But the blessing indicates freedom and agency for the coming child. Better to be a "wild ass" than meek and confined. Better to "live at odds" with others than to eternally submit to abuse as Hagar is being told to do. Blessings come in all shapes and sizes.

After this astonishing blessing from God, Hagar does one of the most astonishing things in Scripture: she names God. Biblical scholar Phyllis Trible points out that while many people in Scripture call *on* God's name, Hagar is the only person in the Bible to *call* God's name—to give God a name.[2] God has given Hagar's child the name "God hears" (Ishmael), and Hagar gives God the name "God who sees" (v. 13).

On its surface, the name that Hagar gives God is a term of praise; it's an acknowledgment of God's power and omniscience. I wonder, though, if there is also a hint of challenge in this name that Hagar so boldly gives to the God of her oppressors. God does, indeed, see. God sees the abuse Hagar has suffered, the desperate state she is in, the dangers her child—and others like him—will face in the world. In naming God as *the one who sees*, Hagar calls God to be accountable for what is seen; she demands that God not turn a blind eye to suffering.

This enslaved woman who, theoretically, has very little power in the world engages in arguably the most powerful act any human in the Bible undertakes: naming God. And her power continues in the naming of her son, Ishmael. The text says that Abram named Ishmael, but we should note that Abram gives the child the name that was revealed to Hagar in the wilderness. This means that either Abram also had a divine messenger visit him and tell him the name or, more likely in my mind, that Abram offered the name that Hagar told him to give the child.

In naming God and her son, Hagar claims power in a society that works to keep her submissive. Naming is a powerful thing. As the first human discovered, places that feel like the wilderness can suddenly become much more manageable, much easier to navigate, when we give names to the creatures we encounter there. Names allow us to praise and to challenge; they define relationships and orient us in unfamiliar spaces.

CONNECT

Have a conversation with a friend or family member about naming. You might discuss the stories behind your own names or times when you have given names (to people, pets, cars, and so on).

CONSIDER

Hagar receives a rather odd blessing in the wilderness. What "mixed blessings" have you received throughout your life?

WEDNESDAY
HAGAR CAST OUT

READ

Genesis 21:8–14

REFLECT

While Hagar claims the power to name God in Genesis 16, God changes Abram and Sarai's names in chapter 17. By chapter 21, Sarah has given birth to Isaac, which makes Hagar's son Ishmael a threat to Isaac's status as the sole heir to Abraham's wealth.

Here we see Sarah continue her abuse of Hagar by demanding that Abraham send her away. Sarah's abusive greed and jealousy likely stem from her own past experiences of abuse and trauma and are fueled by fear for the security of herself and her son. Whatever the reasons for Sarah's demand, Abraham obliges and casts Hagar out. Surely both Abraham and Sarah realize that Hagar and Ishmael's chances for survival will be slim outside of their household.

The first time we see Hagar in the wilderness, she goes there by choice, running away from Sarai's abuse. This time, Hagar does not leave of her own accord but is kicked out with only some bread and a skin of water. Forced to leave her home, Hagar returns to the place that previously offered her refuge.

While leaving Abraham's home is forced upon her, going to the wilderness seems to be Hagar's choice—and it is an interesting choice. I wonder why she took this risk. She could have gone to a city, where there were opportunities to beg or do sex work or otherwise try to earn some support for herself and her child. Or rather than "wandering about" in the wilderness, she could have attempted to travel *through* the wilderness back to her home country of Egypt.

What is it, I wonder, that draws Hagar to the wilderness? At this stage of her life, with all she has experienced, does she fear the abuse of other people more than the harsh conditions of the desert? Given her past experiences, does she consider the wilderness a likely place to encounter God? Does she believe she has the skills to survive there? That her son will be safest if he is far removed from people who wish him ill?

Sometimes the wilderness is a place we end up because we're forced to be there; but sometimes, like Hagar, we choose the wilderness. Perhaps because it seems like the best of many bad options. Or because we trust ourselves to be able to navigate it well. Or because we hope for an encounter with God, and we believe the wilderness is the best place to experience that.

Most often, even if we expect that the wilderness may hold some blessing for us, we will not choose it if "home" is an option. If there is a place for us to be that is familiar and safe *enough* and comfortable *enough*, then we will likely stay there. And if we can't stay there, we'll be tempted to find a place most like it—just as Hagar could have found another city, other people who would use her labor and her body in exchange for some meager sense of security.

Sometimes we are tempted to go back to an earlier home—as Hagar could have gone back to Egypt. We don't know what her life was like there, but we know that somehow she ended up enslaved, presumably because somebody sold her. So we can assume that Egypt was not the healthiest environment. But it was familiar, and she could have tried to go back. Just like we, if forced out of our current place of familiarity, might seek old comforts—even unhealthy ones.

So what makes Hagar head to the frightening possibilities of the wilderness rather than the known and comfortable violence of her current or previous homes? Surely, in part, it is her bravery and self-assuredness. And surely, in part, it is her previous experience in the wilderness. Whatever dangers the wilderness holds, she also knows that God—the God who sees—is there as well. Maybe she risks the wilderness because she feels an obligation to find a better way for her son.

In the end, we don't know *why* Hagar chooses the wilderness. We just know that the wilderness is where she heads with some bread, a skin of water, and her child. It is a dangerous choice. It is also a brave and hope-filled choice. When we are forced from home, may we likewise head toward faith instead of fear.

CONNECT

Join Hagar in her wandering by using the labyrinth image on page 12. Use your finger to prayerfully trace the path from the entrance to the center. Breathe in God's presence as your finger rests in the center, then slowly trace the path back out.

CONSIDER

When, for whatever reason, "home" is no longer a place you can be, what are the familiar but not particularly healthy places you are tempted to go? What wilderness might you wander in instead? How will you have the courage to head toward the wilderness?

THURSDAY
HAGAR ENCOUNTERS GOD

READ

Genesis 21:15–21

REFLECT

Hagar's wilderness wandering has led her to a desperate place. She has run out of water and cannot see a way for herself and her son to survive much longer. She feels powerless to save Ishmael and doesn't want to watch him die, so she places him under a bush and utters one of the most heartbreaking lines in Scripture: "Do not let me look on the death of the child" (v. 16).

Nobody should have to watch their child die. Hagar cannot bear to witness Ishmael's suffering, but she also cannot bear to leave him completely alone in death. After she places him under the bush, she goes "a good way off," but she doesn't walk away (v. 16). It would have been so easy, too easy, to lose herself in the wilderness; to walk and wander until Ishmael was completely lost to her. But she stays with him even though she can't bear to be with him.

And she weeps. She has established a physical distance between herself and her son, but the emotional tie remains strong. Her grief pours out in her voice. Apparently Ishmael, "about the distance of a bowshot" away (v. 16), also cries out. Imagine their sounds of grief and despair meeting and mingling in the space between them. In the physical landscape of wilderness, mother and son experience an emotional wilderness and create a wilderness of sound that reaches beyond them to whoever or whatever might be listening.

God hears their cries. The Bible specifically says that "God heard the voice of the boy," and I wonder if that is an indication of God's mothering heart, that the cries of the child ring stronger and louder than others. In motherly solidarity, God speaks to Hagar through a heavenly messenger: "Do not be afraid, for God has heard the voice of the boy" (v. 17).

The last time Hagar was in the wilderness, she gave God a name: *El-roi*, God who sees (16:13). Now she learns that God is also One who hears. In Exodus, God will hear the cries of the Hebrew people who are enslaved in Egypt; here in Genesis, God hears the cries of two Egyptian people who were enslaved by Hebrews. While Hagar's mothering heart could not bear to see the death of her child, God, with mothering love, both sees and hears the pain of Hagar and Ishmael.

God sees, hears, and responds. "Lift up the boy and hold him fast," the angel tells Hagar (21:18). While Hagar might feel that she needs to distance herself from her son's pain, God assures her that she is strong enough to hold the boy, to see and hear him just as God sees and hears and holds Hagar.

Thankfully, Hagar will not have to see Ishmael die, because in addition to telling Hagar to go to her son, God also reveals the presence of water, thereby giving Hagar a concrete way to save herself and Ishmael from death. I find it fascinating that this well of water has apparently been nearby all along. The text doesn't say that God provided the well—it says that God *opened Hagar's eyes* so she could see the well. Hagar's God is a God who sees and a God who helps her see; this vision saves her life.

I wonder whether it wasn't, in the end, Hagar's inability to watch her son die that ultimately saved them. Was the camouflaged well "about the distance of a bowshot" from the bush that Hagar placed Ishmael under? If she had stayed next to him, would she have been able to see the well, no matter how wide open her eyes were? Perhaps her fear, grief, and weakness lead her to the well in the wilderness. And of course, once she sees the well, her fear and grief subside as her strength returns. She fills the skin with water, crosses the wilderness expanse to her son, and gives him a life-saving drink.

When we think of the wilderness, we are most likely to imagine the opening of this scripture: that the wilderness is a place of despair and grief and pain. Which it sometimes is. But the concluding scene of this scripture also takes place in the wilderness: a scene of connection and sustenance and hope.

This is not a one-time water provision. Now that Hagar has seen the well, she knows where it is. She can go back and get water whenever they need it. This place that Hagar thought would be the death of her turns out to be a place where she and her son will live and thrive for years to come.

CONNECT

Spend some time in contemplative prayer, listening for what God might have to tell you (rather than you telling God all the things). After an extended time in silence with God, open your eyes and look around to discover what God may want to show you.

CONSIDER

Whom do you know (or know of) who is suffering right now? What grief is it difficult for you to witness? Is there a well nearby—some resource to help you support those who are suffering?

FRIDAY
HAGAR ENDURES

READ

Genesis 25:12–18

REFLECT

We tend to think of the wilderness as a place to get through, a place we wander around in for a while until we can find our way home. But what if the wilderness *is* home?

The first time Hagar finds herself in the wilderness, God tells her to return to the household of Sarai and Abram. But the second time Hagar goes into the wilderness, it seems that she and her son settle there. Genesis 21:20–21 repeats for emphasis that Ishmael "lived in the wilderness. . . . He lived in the wilderness." For Ishmael and Hagar, the wilderness becomes their home, not a place they have to endure on their way home.

For those with structural advantage and power, "wilderness" tends to have negative connotations. But for those who are oppressed, the wilderness may not be such a scary place—perhaps not as frightening or dangerous as "civilized" society. The wilderness becomes Hagar's safe place, her sacred space. It is where she finds refuge and where she meets God. It becomes her home.

What might it mean, I wonder, for the wilderness to be our home? For Ishmael and Hagar, it means they are no longer enslaved. They have a new measure of power and control over their lives, over their bodies. They also have a new measure of responsibility for their own survival; they must provide their own food, shelter, and protection.

One way they provide for themselves in the wilderness is to create their own community. Hagar eventually brings another Egyptian woman into the wilderness to be Ishmael's wife. And with his wife, Ishmael creates a family—a community of people who can support one another and help each other survive.

We might think of the wilderness as a lonely space, but it is often a space where we desperately need, and therefore find, other people. It becomes a place where relationships deepen and community is built. Many LGBTQIA people who have been rejected by their families of origin find themselves part of chosen families that provide nurture, safety, and joy in the wilderness. For me, when I entered the wilderness of parenting, my illusions of self-sufficiency went out the window. Reaching out to others for help during some of the most intense parenting challenges strengthened my relationships and helped form a community.

Like Hagar and Ishmael, those who make their home in the wilderness today survive in unexpected ways. People who face displacement, disorientation, and struggle are forced to create and rely on community to survive. They also may need to function outside the parameters of "normal" jobs or family or consumption. The wilderness is a difficult place to live, but in facing the challenges of the wilderness, we can learn to live in creative and life-giving ways.

Hagar and Ishmael do not merely survive in the wilderness, they thrive. In today's reading from Genesis 25, we learn that God has indeed fulfilled the promise that God made earlier to greatly multiply Hagar's offspring (16:10). In fact, Ishmael has twelve sons—"twelve princes according to their tribes" (25:16). These twelve tribes of Ishmael, the descendants of Hagar, are born *a generation before* the twelve tribes of Israel. God fulfills the promise through Hagar's son Ishmael before God fulfills the promise through Sarah's son Isaac.

Hagar's descendants do not stay in the wilderness forever. At the end of today's reading, the author tells us that Ishmael's "descendants settled from Havilah to Shur" (v. 18). They cease their wilderness wandering and settle into a new home. Sometimes in our own periods of disruption and discomfort, we suddenly realize that we are no longer disoriented and uncomfortable. Sometimes, when we live in the wilderness long enough, when we face its challenges and welcome its blessings, it transforms from wilderness to home right under our aching feet.

CONNECT

Whom do you consider the matriarch of your family? How many of her descendants can you name? If she is still living, reach out to her with a visit, phone call, or card.

CONSIDER

Is there a part of your life that feels like you have made a home in the wilderness? Some aspect that is outside what many would consider normal or desirable, but that you have made peace with and maybe even come to love? What helps you thrive in this wilderness?

SATURDAY
HAGAR MISUNDERSTOOD?

READ

Galatians 4:21–31

REFLECT

This passage presents troubling antisemitic sentiments, not to mention an inaccurate and unfair portrayal of Hagar along with problematic allegorization of women's reproductive realities. To be honest, I don't like this passage, and I didn't want to include it in this book. But we are in the wilderness, right? And we are being brave with the questions we ask and the answers we consider, so I invite us to approach today's text with curiosity rather than fear.

The apostle Paul wrote these words to churches in Galatia—groups that he helped start and that were now struggling with various issues of faith and community life. In this letter, Paul addresses a key question of the early church: Do Gentile followers of Jesus need to be circumcised according to Jewish law? This passage, along with many other parts of Galatians, presents Paul's answer to that question: a resounding no.

Paul insists that all followers of Jesus are children of the promise, not of flesh; they are residents of Jerusalem above, not subject to the laws of the earthly Jerusalem. In Jesus, all people are free in the Spirit, not enslaved by the law.

I appreciate what I think Paul is trying to say here; what I find problematic is his oversimplified rhetoric. The complex characters of Hagar and Sarah do not easily fit into the neat and distinct categories in which Paul tries to place them.

Paul presents Hagar as representative of slavery while Sarah represents freedom. But by the end of her story, Hagar was a free woman and the matriarch of a large family. And while Sarah was not technically enslaved, parts of her story remind us that, as a woman, she was essentially the property of her father and then her husband. "Freedom" and "slavery" are not permanent states or clearly defined terms.

Paul also contrasts Ishmael as a "child of flesh" with Isaac as a "child of promise." Yet the biblical account of Isaac's birth confirms that it was, in fact, a birth "of the flesh." The story contains references to Sarah's menopausal state and, according to the translation by biblical scholar Dr. Wilda Gafney, her "wetness"—her sexual pleasure.[3] Ishmael, while certainly a "child of flesh," is also a "child of promise." Remember Genesis 16:10: "I will so greatly multiply your offspring that they cannot be counted for multitude."

It also seems that Paul presents a dichotomy here in which flesh is bad and promise is good; yet these concepts get complicated in Paul's writings. Just a bit before today's reading, Paul reminds us that Jesus was born "of a woman" (Galatians 4:4). This means Jesus was of the flesh. Yet Jesus was also, surely, of the promise. And so these concepts are not as distinct from each other as the Hagar/Sarah analogy might suggest.

Even the scripture that Paul quotes complicates the analogy. As support for the fact that Sarah, the free woman, is "our mother," Paul quotes from Isaiah 54: "Shout for joy, O barren one who has borne no children. . . . For the children of the desolate woman will be more than the children of the one who is married" (v. 1). The thing is, Sarah was not barren forever. And if we had to choose "desolate" as a label for one of the women, it would more aptly be applied to Hagar, who, it turns out, had more grandchildren than Sarah.

While the analogy itself is problematic, I do think the story of Hagar supports the overall point that Paul wants to make in Galatians: that God brings people into relationship with the divine in unconventional ways, and that those relationships are based on faith, not birth. Hagar's story supports Paul's insistence that God desires all people to be free—even if experiencing that freedom means we must spend some time, or a lifetime, in the wilderness.

CONNECT

Read a bit more of Paul's letter to the Galatians. I suggest reading the entirety of chapters 3 and 4, if not the whole book!

CONSIDER

Choose one set of "opposing" categories that you tend to put people in (i.e., Christian/non-Christian, conservative/liberal, rich/poor). How might these categories be more complicated than you sometimes acknowledge? How do they overlap? How do people defy fitting neatly into one or the other?

Blessing for the Second Sunday of Lent: Hagar's Blessing

I see we have found ourselves together
in the wilderness.
Those of you who are fleeing
and those who've been cast out;
those passing through
and those settling in—
whatever brings you here,
I'm glad to be your companion for a time.
I can show you the secret spots of shade,
    but you will have to decide that it's okay to rest.
I can take you to the hidden wells,
    but you will need to draw the water.
I can show you where I met God,
    but I doubt the Holy One will show up for you in exactly that same
        place.
I can breathe along beside you in the silence,
    but you will have to open your own soul to the presence of the divine.
    You will need to speak your own name for God.

It is good, my friend, to be here with you.
Please allow me to offer this blessing for your wilderness journey:
    May your wells be full.
    May your life be free.
    May your love be fierce.
Amen.

BY THY HELP
—
Women Who Save Moses

MONDAY
SHIPHRAH AND PUAH SAVE LIVES

READ

Exodus 1:8–21

REFLECT

In the wilderness, it can seem like there are no good options. Every direction looks like the wrong direction. Every choice carries the potential of a different terrible consequence.

This is exactly the kind of wilderness that the Hebrew midwives Shiphrah and Puah find themselves in. Their king, the pharaoh, gives them an unbelievably horrific command: that they kill the male infants they help deliver. Asking *midwives* to kill babies disrespects and dismisses the vocation and identity of these women who are committed to nurturing life.

Did the pharaoh honestly expect the two midwives to betray their people and their vocation by killing male children? It's almost unthinkable that they would do such a thing, and Pharaoh's request reveals his egotism and shortsightedness.

We see Pharaoh's shortcomings again in the conversation he has with the midwives. He asks them why they haven't killed the baby boys—which should be obvious to anyone. And he accepts their answer: Hebrew women are so "vigorous" that the midwives can't get to the births in time to kill the babies (v. 19). Verse 10 says that Pharaoh wants to deal "shrewdly" with the Israelites, but in the end the Israelite midwives deal shrewdly with him. Anyone who has given birth—or closely supported someone giving birth—understands how ridiculous Shiphrah and Puah's answer is. No matter how "vigorous" the woman, labor generally lasts for hours. But apparently Pharaoh has kept his distance from the messiness of childbirth. He accepts the midwives' explanation and moves on to plan B—which is a plan to kill the male Hebrew children without the assistance of midwives.

I have long admired Shiphrah and Puah, both for what they do and for what they refuse to do. First, they simply refuse to do the terrible thing that Pharaoh tells them to do. Their deliberation process is not recorded, so we don't know how difficult this decision was for them. But in the end, their fear of God is greater than their fear of Pharaoh; their love of life is greater than their desire to protect their own particular lives.

Second, they skillfully engage in conversation with Pharaoh when he confronts them about their inaction. It's possible that the words they say—this explanation that is a non-explanation—simply came to them in the moment. But I like to imagine the midwives having a strategic planning session. When they were told that the pharaoh wanted to have a word with them, they got together and talked about what answer they could give to the pharaoh to keep him from killing them or forcing them to kill others.

"We could just tell him that we absolutely refuse to kill anyone and tell him where he can shove his royal commands."

"We could feel out how serious he is about this whole 'kill all the boys' thing and agree to do it if we absolutely have to."

"We could play dumb and act like we don't remember getting the original memo."

"We could run away and hope he never finds us."

"*Or* we could come up with some explanation that involves the intimacies of women's bodies and childbirth that would make him super uncomfortable and want to just get out of the conversation as quickly as possible."

Whether by strategy or momentary inspiration, Shiphrah and Puah find a way to navigate the situation that does not end in their killing or being killed. They use Pharaoh's cultural and gender-based prejudices to escape punishment for not obeying his orders. The midwives know that he views the Hebrew people as fundamentally "other;" they know that he views women in general as objects for bearing children. So they wisely conclude that he will believe this explanation that makes Hebrew women sound like animals.

The actions of these midwives brilliantly illustrate what it can mean to live out Jesus' encouragement to be wise as serpents and innocent as doves (Matthew 10:16). Shiphrah and Puah are innocent; there is no blood on their hands. And they are wise, using the prejudices of the powerful pharaoh against him. Serpents, after all, fare quite well in the wilderness.

CONNECT

The midwives believed that Pharaoh was a force that should be resisted. What is one force in our world today that God calls us to resist? Look up information on one or two organizations that are actively resisting that force.

CONSIDER

When have you been asked (or simply expected) to do something that you felt was morally wrong? How did you deal with that situation? How does your faith—your "fear of God"—help you navigate difficult wilderness spaces where it seems like there is no good choice?

TUESDAY
JOCHEBED SAVES MOSES

READ

Exodus 1:22–2:10

REFLECT

I find it ironic that Pharaoh orders the male babies to be killed when it is women giving him all the trouble. In these beginning chapters of Exodus, women shine as forces for life in the face of Pharaoh's orders of death. First the midwives defy him and refuse to kill the male babies. Now three women join forces to circumvent his decree that all male babies be drowned in the Nile River. We will get to Pharaoh's unnamed daughter and Moses's sister Miriam later. For now, we turn our attention to Jochebed.

Jochebed is Moses's mother—though we don't learn her name until Exodus 6, and it only shows up one other time in all of Scripture. It's a shame, really, that she's not given more attention, because she truly is a remarkable woman. She finds herself in the deep emotional wilderness of having the life of her baby threatened, and rather than resign herself to Pharaoh's decree, she finds a way to save her son.

First, she hides her baby for three months. Can you imagine? It must have been a terrifying time. Anyone who heard or saw the infant could have reported him—or even taken it upon themselves to drown the baby. With oppressive powers in place, it is difficult to know who you can trust; even Jochebed's Hebrew neighbors could have alerted Pharaoh to the baby's presence.

In this dangerous atmosphere, Jochebed somehow forms an alliance with Pharaoh's own daughter to protect the child. It is possible that the princess randomly finds the baby in the river, but I'm increasingly inclined to believe that the whole situation was orchestrated by Jochebed from the very beginning.

63

For years, I had it in my mind that Moses's mother just put his little crib boat in the rushing river and he randomly landed near the princess. That's usually how the story goes in children's Bibles and movies, but that's not what Scripture says. It *says* she "placed [the basket] among the reeds" (Exodus 2:3). Jochebed sets the basket where the reeds will hold it safely in place. And perhaps she knew—probably she knew—that the princess frequently bathed there.

It may magnify our perception of God's power in this story if we believe that baby Moses just *happens* to float by while Pharaoh's daughter is bathing. But this chance-driven version of the story diminishes Jochebed's intelligence and power and faithfulness. Too often we tell women's stories (and the stories of others who are oppressed) in ways that overlook their agency in order to create feel-good narratives for those with more status and power.

I think about the version of Rosa Parks's story that I was told growing up: that she was a poor, hardworking woman who was just too tired to stand on the bus and so inadvertently propelled the civil rights movement forward. Only later did I learn that she was highly trained in methods of nonviolent resistance; that her refusal to give up her seat on the bus was not the oblivious action of an exhausted woman, but part of a strategic plan to inspire the Montgomery bus boycott and overturn Jim Crow laws.

Sometimes, in the wilderness, we fumble around and find our way by the sheer grace of God. And sometimes God empowers us to plot and plan and subvert the powers of oppression and death to make a more life-giving way for ourselves and others.

I believe Jochebed deserves more credit than she's often given in this story. Credit for her passion and compassion; credit for all she risked in hiding and then releasing her son; credit for her savvy plan to save her son in a way that would guarantee his survival. She deserves credit for the amazing way she navigates her wilderness: with a deep trust in God and an unapologetic resistance to the powers of death.

CONNECT

Do a little internet digging to learn about the story of an activist or action for justice that you admire. Better yet, talk with an activist you know and ask them about the strategizing and planning that happens behind the scenes.

CONSIDER

Somehow, Jochebed was able to plan and carry out a life-saving action despite the fear and stress of her situation. What helps you find calm and focus in times of stress? How can you allow God to lead you through the wilderness?

WEDNESDAY
PHARAOH'S DAUGHTER SAVES MOSES

READ

Acts 7:17–22

REFLECT

Stephen, a leader in the early church, was arrested and brought before the religious council. In his (ultimately unsuccessful) defense, he gives a sweeping summary of Jewish history from Abraham through Solomon building the temple. In his entire fifty-two-verse speech, Stephen mentions only one woman, who is not even Jewish: Pharaoh's daughter.

We can add this unnamed character to our list of women who participate in saving the life of the hapless baby Moses. Like Shiphrah and Puah and Jochebed, this princess was likely in her own kind of wilderness. I will grant you that any wilderness that involves leisurely bathing with attendants and maids is fundamentally different from the wilderness of slavery and threats of genocide. I'm not trying to make false equivalencies here. Still, it's worth acknowledging the disorientation and frustration that people can experience when their own values differ substantially from those of the people around them; when people in their community—in their own family—take actions they understand to be harmful, even evil.

What is a princess to do when her dad, the pharaoh, orders the drowning of every male Hebrew baby?

Biblical scholar Dr. Wilda Gafney makes a strong case for Pharaoh's daughter as an *ally* of the oppressed Hebrew people.[4] One can imagine that the princess was aware of and concerned about the Hebrew's situation by her response to finding the baby in the reeds. She immediately recognizes that he is a Hebrew baby. As she stands there in the Nile River with this baby, she surely knows that her father has commanded that "every son that is born to the Hebrews you shall throw into the Nile" (Exodus 1:22).

It would be so easy, logistically speaking, for her to simply toss the baby downstream and be done with it. But instead she takes pity on him. Moses's sister conveniently shows up and offers to get a Hebrew wet nurse for the baby, and the princess readily agrees.

Can we take a moment to realize how odd this is? How suspiciously convenient that a young Hebrew woman shows up at just that moment with the perfect person to serve as nurse to the baby pulled from the reeds. And how blissfully unsuspecting the princess seems as she readily accepts the offer. Biblical scholar Shana Green suggested to me that Pharaoh's daughter and Jochebed schemed together to arrange for Moses's survival. In our conversation, Green noted the creative ways that they have seen oppressed people, most notably Black women, form alliances and act for liberation. Green believes it unlikely that Jochebed would have risked her baby's life with a random trip down the river—yet entirely possible that Moses's mother would have formed an alliance with the princess. The two women could have planned when and where the desperate mother could leave the baby so the princess could "find" him, and they could have discussed how to allow Jochebed as much access to her child as possible without getting the baby killed. The more I think about the baby in the reeds, the more likely it seems that his rescue was well-planned rather than simply fortuitous.

I would also love to know more about the princess's relationship with her father, the pharaoh. Did she question him to his face or only by her actions? Did she know that he would tacitly go along with her strange adoption, or did she fear he might kill the child despite her intervention? Did her defiance cause a rift in their relationship, or was it already strained?

Relational difficulties are often the biggest stumbling block for me when I desire to be an ally. If I tell my uncle that his joke is racist, will I still get invited to next year's Thanksgiving dinner? If I question my company about gender equality, will I be labeled a troublemaker? If I insist on respectful terms and correct pronouns in relation to LGBTQIA people, will others roll their eyes and avoid conversations with me? To risk damaging relationships with friends, coworkers, and family is no small matter. The princess puts herself in a potentially lonely space: while her sympathies lie with the Hebrew people, she is not (and cannot be) one of them. Yet in defying her father's command and acting on behalf of the Hebrew people, she removes herself from full inclusion in her own family and household. She is, indeed, in a wilderness space.

While Pharaoh's daughter is the only woman mentioned in Stephen's speech, she is also the only woman who saves Moses who is not named in Scripture. We know her position in society and her role in the story, but she does not have a distinct personal identity. Maybe we know the names of the other women because Moses's adoptive mom, the princess, passed these names on to him, telling the child stories of the Hebrew women whose wisdom and courage made his life possible.

When we are in the wilderness, it is easy to lose perspective, to forget the privilege we have because we are so concerned about the difficulties we face. But even in the wilderness—maybe especially in the wilderness—we are called to recognize our privilege, approach others with compassion, and risk our own status and relationships to work as accomplices for justice.

CONNECT

The story we are moving toward in this Lenten season is ultimately a story of God's power and love in the face of the world's injustice. Make a list of people you know (or know of) who are working for justice. Pray for them and for the work they are doing.

CONSIDER

What experiences have you had in working with allies? How were they helpful, and what was frustrating? When have you tried to act as an ally? What have you learned through those experiences?

THURSDAY
ZIPPORAH SAVES MOSES

READ

Exodus 2:15–22; 4:24–26

REFLECT

The relationship between Moses and his first wife, Zipporah, begins at a well—a place of respite in the wilderness. Moses is there because he is running away from Pharaoh, who wants to kill him. Zipporah is there with her (six!) sisters to get water for their father's sheep. For Moses, the well is a place of safety. For Zipporah, it is a place of provision, a place to find the water necessary for life in the wilderness.

On the surface, the story in Exodus 2 is about Moses saving Zipporah and her sisters. He comes to their defense against the bullying shepherds and helps them get water for their sheep. It's a scene straight out of a teen romance movie (if the movie took place in the ancient Near East). But while Moses saves Zipporah from whatever imminent danger the shepherds pose to her, *she* ultimately saves *him* for the longer term by connecting him to her family through marriage.

When Moses meets Zipporah, he is in exile from his homeland of Egypt. I imagine his adoptive mother, the princess, did all that she could to keep Moses safe and included in the royal family. But after he kills an Egyptian, she can't protect him anymore. Pharaoh wants Moses dead (again), so Moses heads into the wilderness, and eventually "he settled in the land of Midian and sat down by a well" (2:15).

Moses's situation in Midian is unclear. He could be fully settled with a house and some land, but it seems more like the extent of his settling in Midian is sitting down by the well. Which isn't very settled. Moses is in a foreign land, separated from family, and in fear for his life. When Reuel gives Zipporah to Moses as his wife, Moses suddenly has a home and a family again. Sure, Pharaoh still wants him dead, but now Zipporah and her entire household are supporting and protecting him.

Not only does Zipporah give Moses a home, she also gives him an occupation. He becomes a shepherd, like her. As a shepherd, Moses spends a lot of time in the wilderness, and it is in the wilderness, while Moses is tending sheep, that God speaks to him through the burning bush (Exodus 3).

After Moses's little chat with God-in-the-bush, he heads back to Egypt to confront Pharaoh, taking Zipporah and their children with him. It is on this journey through the wilderness from Midian to Egypt that we have this baffling story in Exodus 4: "The LORD met him and tried to kill him" (v. 24). Supposedly the "him" is Moses, and God's reasons for trying to kill him are unfathomable. Because God has just spent a lot of time and energy convincing Moses to go to Pharaoh and demand that the Hebrew people be set free. Plus, God taught Moses all those cool tricks and gave him the special staff. It does not make sense that God would now try to kill him.

Maybe the author is confused, or the translation is off, or . . . I don't know what's going on with God and Moses here. But I do know that, once again, a woman comes to Moses's rescue when his life is in danger—and this time Moses isn't a helpless baby, but a grown man.

Zipporah circumcises one of their sons with a sharp rock and touches "his" (presumably Moses's?) feet with the foreskin and says, "Truly you are a bridegroom of blood to me!" (v. 25). Somehow this action and these strange words thwart God's attempts to kill Moses. It is a curious story, and it's difficult to read it as a factual account. Nevertheless, it is testimony we have in Scripture that adds Zipporah to the list of women who save Moses.

Circumcision was generally performed by priests, so with her action Zipporah steps into a priestly role, a role she has apparently inherited from her father. She functions as a priest both in the concrete act of circumcising her son and in intervening between Moses and God. Her priestly action appeases God and saves Moses.

And what does it mean that Moses is a "bridegroom of blood" to Zipporah? That their bodies are connected through sexual intercourse and through having children together. That they share Hebrew blood—their fates are tied to each other and to all who are being oppressed because of their ethnicity.

While the specific action that Zipporah takes here seems odd, we can appreciate the characteristics she displays. This story affirms that Zipporah is a woman who could help keep Moses safe and partner with him in the work God sent him to do. She is the kind of companion you want to have and the kind of person you want to be in the wilderness: loyal, fearless, and decisive.

CONNECT

Give thanks to God for the people and places that serve as wells for you—places you find protection and provision when you are in the wilderness. Ask God to show you how you can draw from these wells more often. What can you do today to help nourish yourself?

CONSIDER

What are a few of your strongest personality traits? How can these traits be used to support others' well-being and encourage their relationships with God?

FRIDAY
MIRIAM SINGS

READ

Exodus 15:1–21

REFLECT

The Bible says that "Moses and the Israelites sang this song" we read today (Exodus 15:1), but many scholars believe it was originally attributed to Miriam. She is, along with the other Hebrew people, literally in the wilderness at this point of the story. The entire community has fled Egypt at Pharaoh's insistence, but then Pharaoh changes his mind and sends his army after them to capture them and bring them back. Miriam and her people are in a terrifying position with the sea on one side and a charging army on the other. They are trapped with nowhere to go—until . . .

You may have heard this story before. The Red Sea parts and the Israelites walk across on dry land. While Moses holds out his hand to part the waters, Miriam leads the celebration when the people make it safely to the other side. The dancing and singing that Miriam leads are important community-forming acts for these people who will be wandering the wilderness together for the next forty years.

Looking at the song itself, we can see that it fulfills many functions. First, it offers praise to God. That is, after all, why the Israelites left Egypt in the first place—to worship God. Miriam leads the people in praise for who God is and what God has done.

Miriam's song also declares the relationship between God and God's people, the Israelites: they are both the people God redeemed (v. 13) and the people God acquired (v. 16). This stands in opposition to other nations named, such as Philistia, Edom, Moab, and Canaan, who experience terror and dread at the hands of Israel's God. The community's relationship with God and with other nations is central to their identity, and Miriam is key in helping them establish this identity as they begin their wilderness journey.

Finally, Miriam's song recounts what has happened at the Red Sea—how God has saved the people from their enemies. This story is repeated multiple times in Scripture. Exodus 14 relates a prose version, and the story is told in the Psalms, in the Prophets, and in the Epistles. It's an amazing, dramatic tale—a favorite of story Bibles, Hollywood movies, and visual artists. The song itself is one of the oldest biblical texts, which means that Miriam's song is likely the oral basis for these other accounts in Scripture.

This song is noteworthy not only for its content, but also for its exuberance. The women play instruments and dance as Miriam sings. This is a celebration! The people have just witnessed an incredible miracle; they have escaped those who wished them harm; they are free to set their own path and worship their God. The scene on the other side of the Red Sea is one of joyful abandon.

From an outside, privileged perspective, this celebration might seem a bit callous. There are dead Egyptians floating in the sea, and the Israelites are rejoicing. "Horse and rider [God] has thrown into the sea!" sings Miriam (Exodus 15:21). But the Israelites are not joyful because the Egyptians have been killed; they are joyful because they have been saved from lives of slavery. Those in positions of privilege and power can and should seriously consider the moral implications of enacting any kind of violence, even for seemingly positive ends. But those who are oppressed and abused should not be questioned or shamed for rejoicing in their own deliverance.

I think it would do us a world of good if we could more fully embrace Miriam's spirit of celebration. Too often we hold back our joy because we think we don't deserve it, or we worry that it will disappear too soon. The Israelites could have shifted their focus to the struggles that lay ahead of them in the wilderness. They could have been sad about the things they had to leave behind or how the muddy path through the sea ruined their good sandals or any number of problems I'm sure they were facing. But instead, they are led by Miriam in a celebration that unites and brings joy to the community.

CONNECT

What are some of your heart songs? What songs remind you of God's presence, power, and love in different situations? Choose one of those songs to listen to a few times and hold in your heart throughout the day.

CONSIDER

What has God done in your life—personal, family, or church—that is worth celebrating? Even though Lent is traditionally a solemn time, what might it look like to set aside your concerns and spend some time in celebration?

SATURDAY
MIRIAM CHALLENGES MOSES

READ

Numbers 12

REFLECT

In case it's not obvious, the writer(s) of Numbers had an extreme pro-Moses bias: "Now the man Moses was very humble, more so than anyone else on the face of the earth" (v. 3). Today's reading certainly seems to privilege Moses over his siblings, condemning Miriam for daring to criticize her brother. But even as Miriam is criticized, she is also shown to be a powerful prophet and leader in her community.

There is some scholarly disagreement about *why* Miriam challenges Moses, but it is clear *that* she goes with Aaron to confront their brother. In this scene, we see Miriam as an equal with both of her brothers. Considering the inferior role that most biblical women are relegated to, it is surprising how often Miriam is listed with her brothers in Scripture. (See Numbers 26:59; Micah 6:4; and 1 Chronicles 6:3, where Miriam is the only woman named in an extensive genealogy.)

It is not only the biblical writers who recognize Miriam's equality with her brothers—God also appears to regard her as their equal. In a very parental moment, God calls all three of the squabbling siblings into a meeting and speaks to both Aaron and Miriam from a pillar of cloud. Ironically, God's argument for why Moses is a greater prophet seems to be that God speaks directly to Moses whereas God speaks to other prophets through dreams and visions—yet here God is speaking to Miriam directly, placing her on an equal footing with Moses.

For some reason, although God speaks to Miriam *and* Aaron, only Miriam is afflicted with the skin disease. On the surface this may seem biased against Miriam, but in a way it elevates her above Aaron; she is the one held primarily accountable for the action, which might mean that she was the leader, the instigator between the two. And when she is afflicted, both of her brothers intervene on her behalf: Aaron asks Moses to heal her, and Moses makes the same request to God. The three siblings are a unit, sharing power, working together, and caring for each other.

Perhaps the greatest indication of Miriam's high status in the community is the fact that all the people wait for her exile from the camp to be over before they continue their journey. While she is physically removed from the people because of her skin disease, she is still an important part of the community, and they do not move on without her.

We tend to think of Miriam as the big sister watching over her little brother or the young woman dancing and singing at the Red Sea. When we look at her whole story, we can see what a powerful woman she is; and we should note that her power comes from her relationships. As a prophet, she has a great deal of power that emerges from her relationship with God—the fact that God speaks to her and empowers her to speak to the people on God's behalf. She also has power by virtue of her relationship with her brothers. Her greatest power may be the relationship she has with her community as a whole. They clearly love her and will not move on without her.

Among people of faith, power can have negative connotations to the point that the people who would exercise power in the most healthy ways are sometimes reluctant to claim any power at all. But when people are in the wilderness, they look for leaders. We all find ourselves in difficult wilderness situations from time to time, and it feels like our society is firmly planted there right now. When good leaders do not step up, harmful leaders are more than ready to fill the gap. Miriam can serve as an example of how to hold power in faithful ways: by listening to God, working with a team, and maintaining strong relationships with the people.

CONNECT

Today's reading is one of many biblical texts that indicate that God speaks to people in dreams. For the next few nights, offer a question to God as you drift off to sleep. If you remember any of your dreams when you wake up, consider if those dreams might contain a word from God in response to the question you asked.

CONSIDER

Think about someone you believe holds power in a healthy way. What is helpful about their use of power? How is their power connected to relationships they have formed with God and with other people?

Blessing for the Third Sunday of Lent: From the Women Who Save Moses

We serve our God of life
in this world hell-bent on death—
using our power to baffle, disrupt, deter, and thwart
    the forces of violence and oppression
that tend to underestimate us
    over and over again.

On you, whose heart also longs for life,
    we lay our hands.
Over you, who have more power than you know,
    we speak this blessing:
When you face the forces of death,
may you meet their caution with courage,
their shortsightedness with broad perspective,
their ignorance with wisdom,
their fear with generosity,
their solemnity with celebration,
their insistence on scarcity
    with faith in God's miraculous abundance.
May God's song be in your heart
and on your lips (and fingertips)
as you lead and scheme and strive toward true life.
Amen.

WEEK 4

FLAMING TONGUES
—
Women Who Claim Power

MONDAY
MAHLAH, NOAH, HOGLAH, MILCAH, AND TIRZAH DEMAND JUSTICE

READ

Numbers 27:1–11

REFLECT

In the difficulties and dangers of wilderness travel, joining with others along the way can provide support and safety. The Israelites were able to escape slavery by moving as a group, and they navigate the unknowns of their wilderness years by forming a close-knit community.

This tendency toward community in the wilderness is generally a good thing. But there is nothing quite like a wilderness crisis to make people long for strong leaders and clear rules. The more chaotic the external world becomes, the more security and predictability people want within their chosen communities. That often means that when great danger is perceived externally, more injustice is likely to be tolerated internally.

Here in Numbers, the Israelites are literally in a wilderness situation, and the leaders are trying to impose a bit of order through a census and the distribution of the hoped-for promised lands. Moses establishes clear rules for who receives what land, and everyone seems happy to go along and accept their portions. Everyone except Mahlah, Noah, Hoglah, Milcah, and Tirzah, whose portion is nothing because they are daughters instead of sons. They challenge the unjust rules set by leadership, and in doing so they have a lot to teach us about how to confront injustice.

First, the sisters notice the unfair situation. They are paying attention to the census and the land apportionment and recognize that they are being left out. This initial step of noticing injustice is not a given, and it is not as easy as it seems. There is so much to distract us, especially in wilderness times. Leaders are often able to move forward with unjust plans simply because the people most harmed by the plans are not (and in many cases cannot be) paying attention. Rome famously provided "bread and circuses" to distract its citizens who might otherwise have risen up against the empire. Often, of course, those in charge don't have to do anything; people will happily distract themselves. Even when people notice that *something* is happening, they may not have the time or capacity to recognize the true injustice of a situation. When the sisters realized they would not be given an inheritance, they could have simply shrugged their shoulders and thought, "Oh well. That's just how it is." Instead, they recognized that the system was unjust.

Second, the sisters have the courage to approach the powers and name the injustice. They go before Moses, the priest, and "all the congregation" (v. 2). What a stressful situation! They make their case to people who are treating them unfairly, speaking their truth to those whom they have no reason to believe will be receptive to their claims.

Third, they make their request strategically. They do not frame their request as being for themselves, but rather ask for an inheritance *in order to honor their father* (v. 4). This framing of the request might be completely sincere, or the sisters might be saying what they expect Moses will care about the most. Either way, it works! When Moses takes their request to God, God tells Moses in no uncertain terms to give Mahlah, Noah, Hoglah, Milcah, and Tirzah an inheritance.

Finally, God's command doesn't stop there; this is not just a special concession for these particular daughters; the rule will apply to any woman who has no brother. While the daughters of Zelophehad cannot control the outcome of their request, they present it in a way that leads to justice not just for themselves but also for others in a similar situation.

Yet even as we gain some inspiration from these women, we should also look to their story as a cautionary tale. A few chapters later (Numbers 36), some men come to Moses and the other leaders to protest the new rule that says women can inherit their father's property. That dispute gets settled in the women's favor (more or less) as well, but it is important to note that justice will not maintain itself. For every movement toward justice there will be people trying to pull it back.

Those of us who want to work with God for justice in the world need to be observant and courageous, strategic and inclusive. And we also need to be vigilant and tenacious. It is a rare gift that the names of Mahlah, Noah, Hoglah, Milcah, and Tirzah are so well-preserved in Scripture. Let us know their names and learn from their story.

CONNECT

Speaking truth to power is a spiritual practice highlighted in this story of the five sisters as well as the story of Jesus' ministry, arrest, and trials. What truth do you need to speak to what power this week? This practice might involve a phone call, an email, or a personal visit.

CONSIDER

When have you noticed injustice in the past, and how have you responded? What injustice do you notice today? What courage and wisdom do you need to address that injustice? Who is working with you to demand justice?

TUESDAY
DEBORAH LEADS THE PEOPLE

READ

Judges 4:1–16

REFLECT

In the United States today, the percentage of Fortune 500 companies with female CEOs just recently crossed the 10 percent threshold.[5] Currently, only one-quarter of US senators are women. Around the world, Roman Catholic, Orthodox, and many Protestant denominations do not permit women to serve as priests or pastors. And the first forty-six presidents of the United States have been men.[6]

So how in the world did Deborah manage to become both a prophet and a judge among the ancient Israelites? Of the twelve judges named in the book of Judges, Deborah is the only woman *and* the only one who is also a prophet. Somehow she acquires a unique position of both political and religious power in a time when most women were legally the property of men and relegated to working in the private spheres of their households.

Most of the women we are meeting in the wilderness get their power in subversive ways. They form alliances with each other; they subtly manipulate situations; they are sneaky about how they use power so the men around them don't notice. But now we come to Deborah, who surprisingly has real institutional power. She has titles, she has status, she even has a tree named after her! Deborah has the power to summon important people, like the military commander Barak.

Not only does Barak come when Deborah sends for him, not only does he listen to her military advice, but he also insists that she go with him to the battlefield. Deborah's accompaniment of the army seems to be a significant element of this story, because it is repeated and emphasized in the text.

Deborah's going with her people into battle places her in stark contrast to another Israelite leader, King David, who lounges about at home while his soldiers fight (see 2 Samuel 11:1).

Not all leaders live into their responsibility in the same way, but institutional power comes with a great deal of responsibility. A complete lack of institutional power can make you feel powerless, with no choices—which is a particular kind of wilderness feeling. But the abundant choices that come with acknowledged power can also feel like a wilderness.

When you know that people will listen to you, what you say really matters. When you can choose to keep yourself safe while you put others in danger; to keep a disproportionate amount of wealth for yourself; to demand more work from others than you are willing to do—when you have this kind of power, maintaining your integrity is a deep challenge. Those with power often find themselves in a wilderness of overwhelming choice, opportunity, and temptation.

Despite Deborah's power, despite her ability to set the rules and say no, she agrees to accompany Barak on this military mission she has given him. With her significant institutional power, Deborah chooses to exercise power *with* rather than power *over* her people. Instead of giving blanket commands and retreating to safety, she encourages, directs, and accompanies Barak to the battlefield.

Using power with integrity is, of course, important for how we function in the world; it is also important because it informs how we understand God. When the time comes for Barak to lead his soldiers against the army of Sisera, Deborah tells Barak to go, because "Has not the LORD gone out before you?" (Judges 4:14). Just as Deborah is a leader who accompanies her people, so too she understands God to be one who accompanies the people. In Christian belief, this accompaniment of God is fulfilled in the incarnation: Jesus is God among us.

As people of faith, how we use our power can deeply affect how people come to understand God and God's power. *Servant leadership* is a popular term in many church circles, where it is generally associated with the leadership style of Jesus. Yet here in Judges, about a thousand years before Jesus' birth, we have the model of Deborah—a woman with unexpected power who models this same kind of leadership. She sets an example of using power *with* and *on behalf of* her people as she leads with strength and compassion.

CONNECT

Consider a woman in power whom you admire. Through studying or talking with her, learn more about how she came to power and how she hopes to use her power.

CONSIDER

Lent provides an opportunity for us to consider issues of power from a more faithful perspective. How have you experienced people in power? How do these experiences affect how you understand God? What does Jesus' life, death, and resurrection suggest about how God exercises power?

WEDNESDAY
JAEL KILLS SISERA

READ

Judges 4:17–22; 5:24–27

REFLECT

If this were a movie, we could make Sisera a true villain—not just a generic military enemy but a person whom the audience would despise on a very personal level. Given the ferocity of Jael's attack, it seems possible that Sisera has been to her tent before—uninvited. It is entirely possible that Sisera has used his physical strength and societal position to coerce or outright force Jael to have sex with him. He seems quite comfortable coming into her tent and lying down under her rug. He asks for a drink and tells her to keep watch with the complete expectation that she will obey him. All our movie would need is a scene suggesting his sexual violence toward Jael, and the audience would cheer her on as she swings the mallet and forces the tent peg through his temple and into the ground.

It would also be possible to make a movie portraying Jael as the villain. We could show her using numerous men to gain various advantages and favors. She could be a selfish manipulator using Sisera for her own purposes, ultimately murdering him when she decides her interests are better aligned with the Israelites. Perhaps Sisera is a nice guy just doing his job as a military commander and Jael abuses and betrays him in the most terrible of ways.

Strictly on the basis of the biblical text, we cannot know for sure which Hollywood movie version would be most accurate. Surely Jael and Sisera were complex people with both redeeming and problematic qualities; still, I do not believe it is a stretch to see suggestions of some sort of sexual relationship between them. The poetic recounting of Sisera's murder in Judges 5 has strong sexual suggestions: "between her feet he sank, he fell"

(v. 27). Referencing this passage, the Talmud says that Jael had sex with Sisera seven times in order to make him tired enough to fall into a deep sleep (Nazir 23b).

This story ends with a macabre tableaux: a bloody and disheveled Jael standing with a battle-worn Barak gazing down at the mutilated body of Sisera. The two men, both military commanders who are expected to be strong and powerful, have been bested by a woman. Jael kills one commander and does the job the other was unable to accomplish. In this scene we see that the power Jael formed through her relationship with Sisera has proven stronger than Barak's military power.

While I appreciate the idea that relational power is stronger than military power, I remain troubled by the extreme violence of this story. Even though Jael's power is not the military power of Barak and Sisera or the institutional power of Deborah, Jael, like these other three, uses her power to violent ends. There is, it seems, a disturbing relationship between power and violence—one can seek power through violence (and threats of violence), and one can use power already acquired to enact violence at will.

Isn't this a true wilderness? Where violence seems the only conceivable way to gain and to wield power. Where oppressors and oppressed alike are stuck in the cycle of fear and violence. The end of Deborah's song in Judges 5 says that after the defeat of the Canaanite army and the murder of Sisera, "the land had rest forty years" (v. 31). But this is not generally how it works. Violence doesn't lead to peace, but only to more violence.

As much as I love to see a powerful woman, especially in the biblical text, I have to concede that there may be no true hero in this story after all. Perhaps it is not a triumphant story of justice coming to a terrible man or a tragic story of a good man brought down by a bad woman. Maybe it is a story about the suffering that comes to us all when violence is the preferred form of power for some and the only means of power available to others.

CONNECT

Seek a more in-depth understanding of what it means for people to participate in war: talk with a war veteran or read a book or watch a movie about the experience of war.

CONSIDER

Violent acts lead to cycles of violence that can feel like a terrifying, inescapable wilderness. What types of violence are you tempted to commit, and what circumstances make you most likely to give in to that temptation? Remember that not all violence is obvious or physical.

THURSDAY
VASHTI REFUSES THE KING

READ

Esther 1:5–22

REFLECT

This story takes place in what could be considered the opposite of the wilderness: a banquet in the king's palace with gold goblets overflowing with wine and abundant food. Vashti's story begins in the heart of power and luxury, a far cry from the vulnerable starkness of the desert. And the story ends with her banishment into what King Ahasuerus must imagine is a true wilderness. I wonder, though, whether Vashti actually ends up in a more hospitable and solid place than she begins.

It seems that part of being in the wilderness is lacking power—you cannot control the elements, the landscape, the wild animals. And in many ways, Vashti moves *into* power as this story progresses. The first thing we know about Vashti is her title: Queen. This certainly seems to grant her a great deal of power. Deborah's social position of judge and prophet can't even compare with the power behind the position of queen. And, of course, with that title comes extravagant wealth, which affords its own kind of power.

We soon learn, however, that as far as King Ahasuerus is concerned, *he* is the one with ultimate power over the queen. He demands that she come before him "wearing the royal crown" (v. 11) so that he can show off her beauty to his drunk buddies. In asking her to wear the crown, we can see that he also wants to show off his power; he controls royalty. But Vashti does not comply with the king's command. The text doesn't tell us why she refuses to go; there may be a particular reason, or she may simply have had enough with being objectified and ordered around. Whatever the case, she claims a little bit of the power due a queen and says she will not go.

This, of course, enrages the king. He consults with the sages and shifts quickly from granting Vashti little power—assuming she would simply come at his command—to believing the sage's ridiculous overstatement of her power: "This very day the noble ladies of Persia and Media who have heard of the queen's behavior will rebel against the king's officials, and there will be no end of contempt and wrath!" (v. 18).

Vashti's refusal to come before the king will obviously not cause all of the noblewoman around to treat their husbands with contempt. But in this statement we see the unreasonable fear that emerges when those who are supposed to be subservient attempt to exert even the least bit of power. This fear is twofold. First, this fear says that a little bit of power will quickly become overwhelming power; Vasti will soon be ruling the kingdom! And it is coupled with the fear that if those who have been oppressed gain any power, they will use it to harm and oppress those who are currently in power; the noble ladies will treat their husbands with contempt and wrath!

The type of fear that King Ahasuerus exhibits is a constant throughout history. It is the fear that led to Jesus' crucifixion, to the Holocaust, to chattel slavery. It is the fear that opposed women's suffrage and civil rights and marriage equality. "If you give them an inch, they'll take a mile . . . and then use it to destroy us."

This is, in a sense, its own form of wilderness—to live in constant fear of losing any small amount of power; to feel the need to control others so that they will not try to harm you. King Ahasuerus and his sages, despite their drunken revelry, seem in this scene to be quite sad and pitiful men. The kind of men who, in a move that seems truly juvenile and, unfortunately, too familiar today, send out a decree to all the land "declaring that every man should be master in his own house" (v. 22). When you feel the need to declare your power in this way, there's a pretty good chance you've already lost it.

In the end, Vashti retains her power by refusing to come before the king and his buddies. King Ahasuerus tries desperately to assert his power by stripping Vashti of her title and banishing her from his presence. In his mind, I expect he is condemning her to a wilderness existence without access to all the trappings of luxury provided in the palace. But for Vashti, perhaps the banishment is a welcome relief from what she experienced as the wilderness of the palace.

If we could ask Vashti what we can learn from her story, I expect that she would tell us to remember that things are not always what they seem. Luxury can be a wilderness. Being kicked out can be freedom. And it's likely that the more someone insists on performing their power, the less real power they actually have.

CONNECT

Step into the role of Queen Vashti by hosting a banquet. No need for golden goblets and endless wine, but somehow enjoy a special time together with friends amid this stark Lenten season.

CONSIDER

In this week's news headlines, where do you see people's fear of losing power having troubling effects? How might power shift in healthy, peaceful ways?

FRIDAY
ESTHER GUIDES HER PEOPLE

READ

Esther 4

REFLECT

With Vashti removed from her role as queen, King Ahasuerus has a beauty competition and chooses a Jewish woman, Esther, as his new queen. Unaware of Esther's background, the king agrees to let one of his officials, Haman, issue a decree that all the Jews in the kingdom should be killed on a particular day. This is the plan that Mordecai, Esther's cousin and adoptive father, learns about; this is the plan he hopes she can stop.

Mordecai and the other Jews who know of Haman's decree are certainly in a wilderness place—a place where they are fearful and feel powerless. They lie in sackcloth and ashes because they do not know what else to do; the situation is out of their hands, and the only option they see is to turn it over to God. Well, God and Esther.

Esther is the one Jewish person in the kingdom who *might* have the power to stop Haman's plot. So while Mordecai and company are in the wilderness of powerlessness, Esther inhabits an equally challenging wilderness of potential power. Mordecai doesn't have to make a difficult choice, because he doesn't really have any choices to make. There's not much he can do. But *Esther?* Esther has an excruciating choice: whether to risk her own life for the chance to save the lives of her people.

Esther doesn't have the luxury of lying around in sackcloth and ashes; she has to decide what to do. And she does. But first she asks all the Jews to fast and says that she will do the same. With this request, Esther moves into a position of being a spiritual leader in addition to being, at least by title, a political leader. In Scripture, the activities of wearing sackcloth and ashes and fasting are almost always connected to prayer, and it is reasonable

94

to assume that prayer is implied in Esther's instruction that all the Jewish people fast as she prepares to approach the king.

Despite her power as queen, Esther acknowledges God's greater power and calls on God for courage and success in her endeavor. Esther's story is one of recognizing both the extent and limitations of one's power.

It is difficult to accurately assess our power because power is so slippery. There is the official power of position we might have—as a queen, a pastor, a teacher, a boss, a parent, a politician, or any number of roles that come with inherent power. When we inhabit a particular role, we should not ignore the power we have been granted or make excuses for why we can't use that power. Yet no power is absolute. Often, people don't have the full extent of power that those on the outside might think they have. Church power dynamics are complex, and pastors are rarely able to make big decisions unilaterally; politicians have to manage, well, politics; and parents soon find out just how much power a three-year-old can wield.

For those on the outside, it might seem that Esther, as queen, has a lot of power. But she knows how palace politics work. And she knows what happened to Vashti. Her title grants her only so much power; what it mostly gives her is proximity to the king, who has the real power. Still, we should not dismiss proximity—it is a privilege that can easily translate into power. Esther understands this and uses her proximity as power, even as she also leans into the power of God to guide and protect her and her people.

The idea of power in position is highlighted in Mordecai's infamous question to Esther: "Who knows but that you have come to your royal position for such a time as this?" (v. 14 NIV). Mordecai recognizes that Esther's inherent beauty and a confluence of circumstances have put Esther in the place she is in with the opportunity that she—and only she—has to approach the king and stop the planned genocide of her people.

Mordecai's question is one worth asking when opportunities arise: Have you come to be who you are and where you are for "such a time as this"? In the wilderness, we would all do well to recognize the power we have and to acknowledge the limitations of that power. We would do well to call on the presence and protection and power of God when we find ourselves in a place to address a danger or injustice in the world.

CONNECT

People have long engaged in the spiritual practice of fasting during Lent. Decide what you will fast from (not necessarily food) and choose a set amount of time for your fast. How does this experience make you more aware of God's presence?

CONSIDER

Are there areas in your life where you might be underestimating the power you have? Do you have power because of your proximity to certain people? In what areas is your power truly limited?

SATURDAY
ESTHER SAVES HER PEOPLE

READ

Esther 5, 7

REFLECT

Esther does not take her power for granted. Even though she is the queen, she strategically approaches the king to make sure she is heard. She builds up to the big reveal (that she is Jewish) by feeding him and, most likely, flirting with him. She makes sure that he is in a good mood and that she has his full attention before she tells him of the danger posed to her people. She also makes sure that Haman is close at hand.

In many ways, Haman serves as a foil to Esther. While Esther is humble, Haman brags and boasts. Esther seems content with her life even though she is an orphan and a member of an oppressed minority; Haman, despite his wealth, family, and status, complains that he cannot possibly be happy, because Mordecai exists. Esther takes great care when she approaches the king: she takes her time, tends to the king's feelings, and presents a modest request. In contrast, Haman is brash and thoughtless.

From the beginning, Haman cannot read the situation and thinks that Esther's invitation to the dinners is an honor rather than a threat. Once Esther makes her revelation and the king becomes angry, Haman panics; he begs the queen for his life by throwing his body onto hers. When the king comes back into the room, it looks to him like Haman is trying to assault Esther. If the king's little walk in the garden had calmed him down, his rage returns the second he sees Haman sprawled across Queen Esther's couch. Esther's wisdom stands in stark contrast to the foolishness of Haman. It turns out that all the financial and physical and institutional power Haman has is not worth much, because he does not have power over himself.

We also see that the potential limitations of Esther's power—her status as a woman and an ethnic minority—are overcome by her wisdom and self-control. In considering the heroism of Esther, we tend to highlight her bravery—which indeed is commendable. We also often lift up her faith—demonstrated by her request that the people fast as she prepares to approach the king. Sometimes we even note her beauty as one of her heroic traits. But none of these qualities would have allowed her to save her people if it weren't also for her savvy approach to telling the king about the plot.

I imagine that the time of fasting was crucial to Esther's success. We see how poorly things turn out for Haman, who never seems to fully consider the consequences of his attitude and actions. But Esther pauses; between agreeing to approach the king and actually going through with it, she takes time to fast and pray. It is likely during this time that she makes her careful plan: the initial approach, the first dinner, the second dinner, with Haman invited to both meals. I expect she selected her clothing and planned the menus and thought through what she would say.

It turns out that my inability to win beauty pageants isn't the only way I differ from Esther. I also struggle a lot with taking the necessary pauses. Once I've decided to do something, my tendency is to go full steam ahead, getting so caught up in the plan *to* do it that I forget to think about *how to* do it. This is one of many areas where I find that good spiritual practices aren't just good for my spiritual well-being. The practices of Sabbath, prayer, fasting—these pausing practices—give me space to enter into difficult situations with wisdom and a sense of God's leading and presence. The pauses can support my practical planning as well as my spiritual preparedness.

For Esther, the planning in the pauses was literally a matter of life and death. For most of us, the stakes aren't that high, but the pauses still matter. Especially in the wilderness.

CONNECT

What is something, big or small, that you have decided to do? Spend some time praying and planning how you will do it.

CONSIDER

Reflect on a time when you rushed into something and faced negative consequences. What are some ways you could pause between the deciding and the doing to act with more intentionality?

Blessing for the Fourth Sunday of Lent:
From the Women Who Claim Power

We found power in our positions
    and our relationships;
power in our beauty
    and our bodies;
power in our wisdom
    and our skill;
power in our patience
    and our bold action.
We found power in our God,
    who is not only father and king and lord,
    but first breath and womb and mother—
        the breasted God who feeds and strengthens us.

We found our power, and in our best moments
we used our power for the work of God in the world:
    the work of justice
    the work of guidance
    the work of protection
    the work of liberation
    the work of life
    the work of salvation in all its many forms.

May our power empower you
to walk through the wilderness as your full self
    without diminishment
    without apology
    without fear.

May God's power hold and guide you
    through your strength and your weakness
    in all the wilderness places.
Amen.

WEEK 5

TUNE MY HEART
—
Women Who Love

MONDAY
LOT'S WIFE LOVES HER HOME

READ

Genesis 19:1–26; Luke 17:28–33

REFLECT

Even though the biblical text doesn't give this particular woman in the wilderness a name, her story is well known. When Jesus tells his disciples to "remember Lot's wife" (Luke 17:32), there's no need for him to repeat the story. They already know about how this woman, forced to flee her home, looked back toward the city she was leaving and turned into a pillar of salt.

This odd story is almost certainly inspired by the striking salt and dirt pillars that form in the region of the Dead Sea. Yet the story's oversized presence in our tradition suggests that this unnamed woman's action speaks to something deeply human: the compulsion we have to look back, our tendency to love and long for home—even a home as terribly toxic as Sodom. Especially in the wilderness, where Lot's wife most certainly was, it's tempting to want the security of what you know, even if what you know is pretty terrible. I think of the Israelites wandering in the wilderness, longing for the "fleshpots" of Egypt—where they had been enslaved and beaten (Exodus 16:3). I think of foster children I have known who desperately wanted to go back home, even though I knew they had not been treated well there.

It is a human tendency to look back, and the consequences faced by Lot's wife seem harsh. Especially considering that both Lot and his wife go against God's instructions. God's messengers tell Lot to "flee to the hills," and Lot says, "No, I'd rather flee to this town" (see Genesis 19:17–20). The messengers say to Lot and his family, "Do not look back," and Lot's wife does look back. So why is Lot allowed to go to the town he names but his wife is turned into a pillar of salt? It doesn't seem fair. What, really, is so bad about looking back?

Centuries after the story of Lot's wife emerged, Jesus uses it as a sermon illustration. Jesus' teaching suggests that looking back means an unwillingness to embrace the changed life that God is calling us to. Change is difficult even when it is good—even when it is from God. In the Gospels, Jesus often challenges people who hesitate to follow him. He calls fishermen to leave their nets right there at the seashore; he famously says to a would-be-disciple: "Let the dead bury their own dead" (Luke 9:60). And in his Luke 17 sermon, Jesus uses Lot's wife as an example of someone who tries to make her life secure, and thus loses it.

In Luke's version of the teaching, Jesus speaks of trying to make your life "secure" (v. 33). The parallel teaching in John says, "Those who love their life lose it" (12:25). And so it comes back to love. Kind of. Am I allowed to say that I like Luke's version better? Because I don't think Jesus has anything against people loving their lives; Jesus wants us to enjoy and appreciate our lives. I think Luke's version gets closer to what I expect Jesus meant. If we want to be secure, to keep things the same, if we love *the way our lives are right now* too much, then we will be unwilling to move into the life God has for us. We will lose our potential life for the sake of our current, known life.

It's not that we shouldn't love our lives, but it matters *how* we love our lives. And this question of how to love life is a tricky one. A healthy love of life involves both looking back and moving forward. When one's history includes trauma, which there certainly is with Lot's wife and the people of Sodom, it is especially important to acknowledge and process what happened. But it is not healthy to dwell, to let the memories and the concerns for the past thwart our progress into a new future. And it is not healthy to be so afraid of the wilderness journey ahead that we refuse to leave a secure life. It is not healthy to love our lives as they are to the point of losing the lives that God is calling us into.

When we sense God's call away from the familiar and into the wilderness, we are invited to step out in faith. We are invited to make the wilderness journey without regret, focusing on the path that Jesus reveals along the way.

CONNECT

Try a wilderness dot meditation. You will need a piece of paper and a writing utensil. Consider a situation in your life where you think God may be calling you to a time of transition—perhaps some form of security you might need to leave behind. Then simply make dots on your paper (like grains of sand in the desert wilderness) as you talk with God about the situation and what God's call might be.

CONSIDER

How have you struggled to leave unhealthy situations in the past? Is there something you are struggling to leave behind right now? What next steps do you want to take?

TUESDAY
THE WIDOW OF ZAREPHATH LOVES A STRANGER

READ

1 Kings 17:1–16

REFLECT

A drought has left the widow and her son destitute, without enough water or flour or oil to sustain them. I've always thought it cruel of Elijah to even ask her for food and water. Elijah, though, is only doing what God has told him to do, so maybe my complaint here is really with God.

Recently, though, I noticed something odd about this story, something that leads me to a potential alternate reading. In verse 9, God tells Elijah: "I have commanded a widow [in Zarephath] to feed you." But when Elijah gets to the designated town, he doesn't search for a widow with whom God has made him dinner reservations. No. Elijah just calls out to the first random widow he sees. She tells him she doesn't have enough to share with him. Surely if the Holy One had spoken to her and told her to feed Elijah she would have been more agreeable.

So what if . . . just play along with me here . . . what if Elijah went to the *wrong widow*? What if somewhere else in Zarephath there was a wealthy widow with a feast spread out on her table waiting for the prophet to show up? If that's the case, Elijah asking *this widow* for food is both incredibly rude and also life-saving. I don't pretend to know what God's intent was or what Elijah may or may not have gotten wrong in this whole scenario. What I do know is that the widow somehow manages to extend her love beyond her son to include this strange stranger, and her ability to extend that love saves all their lives.

This extension of love is so hard. The wilderness is challenging enough when you are navigating it for yourself; it can be excruciating when you are also responsible for someone else. When the people closest to me are suffering and in danger, I want to devote all my resources to caring for them—all my time, all my money, all my oil and flour and water. How does the widow do it? How does she expand her love to include a stranger during such a desperate time?

In part, I think, she extends care to Elijah because of her trust in God. In response to Elijah's request for food, the widow says: "As the LORD your God lives, I have . . . only a handful of meal in a jar and a little oil in a jug" (v. 12). I tend to read her opening phrase as a mere figure of speech, the way one would say "for real, I promise" to a religious person: "as the LORD your God lives." But what if it's more than that? What if she really means to bear witness to the fact that the God of Elijah is a living God? Perhaps this little turn of phrase reminds the widow of God's life, of God's presence and power. So when Elijah shares God's promise that the meal and oil will not run out, the widow believes it; she trusts in the living God and thus extends her love beyond her own household.

Maybe the widow extends her love to Elijah out of sheer compassion. Here is a man in a situation similar to hers. He must have looked pretty rough after spending all that time by the wadi eating whatever random food the ravens brought him (1 Kings 17:5–6). The widow knows what it feels like to be thirsty, to be hungry, to feel your life dwindle away. She tries to stay focused on herself and her son, but in the end she cannot ignore Elijah's suffering, so she is willing to do what she can for him.

Maybe her trust in God or her deep compassion leads the widow to share what little food she has with Elijah. Or maybe it is sheer desperation. She says that her plan is to make one final meal before she and her son die of starvation. Does it really matter if that final bit of oil and flour is shared three ways instead of two? The end result will be the same. And if there is even the slightest chance that what Elijah says is true—that God will provide food until the drought ends—then she might as well give it a try. Desperation leads people to take all kinds of risks. The widow has nothing to lose by sharing what she has because she already expects to lose everything.

In the wilderness, our tendency is often to keep our heads down and just care for ourselves and our own people. But the desperation of the wilderness can be a grace that leads us to trust in God and have compassion for others.

CONNECT

Make some bread and share it!

CONSIDER

Think about a time when you felt desperate. In what ways did you narrow your focus to yourself and your family? In what ways were you able to extend compassion?

WEDNESDAY
THE WIDOW OF ZAREPHATH LOVES HER SON

READ

1 Kings 17:17–24

REFLECT

Imagine the widow's surprise when she baked the bread for Elijah and realized that there was still enough meal and oil to make some for her son and herself. Imagine her surprise the next morning when there was somehow still enough to make more bread. I wonder how many days it took for her to understand that there would always be enough. How long until she felt a deep sense of relief as she realized that she would not have to watch her son die?

If you've nursed a loved one through a major illness or cared for them as they recovered from a serious injury, you can relate to this sense of relief, to the fog lifting and the slow release of breath as you accept the fact that this one you love will live. So it seems especially cruel that after such tension, grief, and relief, the widow's son would become ill to the point of death.

We can understand the widow's anger. We can understand her impulse to blame her own previous sins and to blame the prophet who was with them through the first ordeal. With her son's illness the widow enters the wilderness of fear, which is a space of heightened and varied emotions. And these emotions—the grief, anger, guilt, and despair—are all intensified because of her deep love for her son. It may not be reasonable for the widow to blame Elijah for her son's illness, but it is understandable.

I find verse 19 especially heart-wrenching: "[Elijah] said to [the widow], 'Give me your son.' He took him from her bosom . . ." She doesn't give the prophet her son; Elijah has to take her son out of her arms. The widow wants Elijah's help, but when he asks for her son's body, she can't seem to let go. The fierceness of her love demands that she hold her beloved close.

Is there a wilderness more profound than the death of a child?

Yet once again, the tragedy that the widow fears does not come to pass. Just as she did not have to watch her child starve, so too this illness that has taken the breath from her son does not lead to his death. The revival of the widow's son is one of the most astounding miracles in the Bible; it's one of only a handful of stories of life being restored. The widow experiences what we all hope for in the wilderness: that our fears will turn out to be unfounded; that we will be wrong about there being no breath— no spirit, no life—left; that the dryness and death we see around us will bloom into life.

It seems strange, and somehow significant, that the widow is not in the room when life comes back into her son. She doesn't see Elijah lay the boy on the bed and stretch out on top of him. She doesn't hear Elijah's desperate prayer. She watches Elijah carry her son's lifeless body up the stairs and then sees the prophet bring her living son back down the stairs. She hears the words "See, your son is alive" and feels the wiggly weight of the boy as Elijah places him in her arms (v. 23).

What joy, what relief she must have felt in that moment. I'm surprised she could even find words to speak to Elijah: "Now I know that you are a man of God and that the word of the Lord in your mouth is truth" (v. 24). She has already been saved from starvation, already seen the power of God to refill the meal and the oil again and again and again. But it takes *this* miracle, it takes life from death, a blooming in the barren wilderness, to convince her that Elijah is a man of God. For the widow, then, as for us today, vibrant life in the wilderness is the surest sign of God's presence.

We must also acknowledge, though, that death does not always give way to (restored earthly) life. Sometimes the meal and oil do run out; sometimes the breath does not return. Sometimes the wilderness truly is as barren and dangerous as we fear. While loving deeply in such harsh conditions may intensify our grief and our pain, such love is also a gift to provide purpose and comfort and joy as we walk through the unknown together.

NNECT

Lent is not only a season to contemplate death; it is also a time of growth. Plant something or tend to some things that have already been planted.

CONSIDER

What wilderness are you in right now? What signs of life do you see?

THURSDAY
A WOMAN LOVES HER BELOVED

READ

Song of Songs 2

REFLECT

Song of Songs stands out in the biblical canon because of its focus on human, rather than divine, love. It may seem strange to discuss romantic love in a Bible study at all, let alone in the middle of Lent, but as we journey through the wilderness with biblical women, Song of Songs is an important text to consider. It is not only God's love that can sustain us in the wilderness; our love for each other is also important as we seek to find a path through uncertainty, as we long for life amid desolation.

While male voices dominate the biblical texts, Song of Songs highlights the voice of a woman. The female speaker in Song of Songs is open about the emotional and physical passion she feels for her beloved. Many biblical stories treat women's bodies as sexual objects to be used by men for male pleasure and for procreation. From Eve to Hagar to Bathsheba to Esther, women's sexuality is presented as being in service to male desire. A few women—such as Tamar, Ruth, and Jael—intentionally use their sexuality to get something they want from men—a baby, a husband, a military conquest. But our poet here in Song of Songs is the only woman I have come across in the Bible who is shown to *enjoy* sex. She takes pleasure in her own body and in the body of her lover.

The poet communicates her pleasure by engaging all the senses. She tastes her lover's sweet fruit (v. 3); she longs for his hands on her body (v. 6); her lover speaks to her of the fragrance of flowers (v. 13); her lover wants to see her face and hear her voice. (v. 14). Their love and longing for each other are immersive and very physical.

This fully embodied love is worth paying attention to as we travel through the season of Lent and contemplate what it means to worship God

113

in the person of Jesus. As Christians who believe in the incarnation—God become flesh—we cannot separate ourselves into distinct categories of *spirit* and *body*; we cannot understand the fullness of love without considering how love touches our bodies as well as our minds and spirits. Human love and divine love are interconnected.

In this particular section of the song, we should note that the woman begins with words of love for herself: "I am a rose of Sharon, / a lily of the valleys" (v. 1). Before proclaiming the beauty of her beloved, she claims her own beauty. Her self-love becomes the foundation of her love for the other. Her love for herself includes appreciation of her body, which in turn leads to her confidence in pursuing her own physical pleasure.

One of the most well-known lines in Song of Songs is from verse 16: "My beloved is mine, and I am his." In a contemporary context, this sounds like a lovely sentiment for a wedding homily or a Valentine's Day card; people have the quote hanging on their walls and engraved in their jewelry. We forget that in many societies of the ancient world, women literally belonged to men—daughters were the property of their fathers, and wives were the property of their husbands. In this context, "My beloved is mine" is a radical statement for a woman to make. Our poet insists that the belonging is mutual; the desire is mutual; the pleasure is mutual; the love is mutual.

Mutuality is a welcome path through the wilderness, which is so often a place of isolation. Sometimes this isolation is a result of being alone, but isolation can also come from relationships of domination. In such relationships, we rightly understand that the person being oppressed suffers. Sometimes we forget that these relationships also take a toll on the oppressor. In such unequal relationships, nobody has a partner; everyone is alone.

The words that the woman's lover speaks to her in this poem promise the end of winter—the end of isolation and barrenness. With love, fully human and embodied love, we can welcome flowers and singing and fruit. With love, we can make our way through the wilderness.

CONNECT

Write a poem that celebrates some form of human love. If writing poetry is not your thing, read some love poems or sing along to some love songs.

CONSIDER

Think about two or three healthy romantic or familial relationships you have observed or been part of. What characteristics did they share? What are some qualities of a healthy relationship?

FRIDAY
A WOMAN LOVES LOVE

READ

Song of Songs 8:1–7

REFLECT

"Many waters cannot quench love" (v. 7). I wonder whether the poet wrote this in response to all the people who tried to throw a wet blanket on her love. There are hints here, and in other parts of Song of Songs, that the two lovers are not supposed to be together. They seem to be sneaking around trying to hide their relationship. The poet longs to be able to kiss her lover in public and take him to her mother's house, but none of those things are possible (vv. 1–2). Instead, the two must meet in the wilderness and make love under the trees. That may be a romantic image on the surface of things, but I expect all the bugs and itchy leaves got really old really fast.

However uncomfortable their forest encounters might have been, the experience of the two lovers can remind us that the wilderness is not always a place of danger and despair. Like Hagar, these two flee *to* the wilderness in order to experience a freedom that is not available to them in the "civilized" world. The wilderness becomes a place to escape societal judgment and be more fully themselves. The wilderness is a place where the lovers can live into the love they share rather than hide their true feelings and pretend to be people they aren't.

While there is no indication that the female speaker of the Song was literally enslaved like Hagar, she was certainly restricted by societal norms. She faced expectations about who she should and shouldn't be with, how she should and shouldn't use her body, what kind of pleasure she was allowed, how she should feel about herself in general and her sexuality in particular. I'm sure there were also expectations about what kind of poetry she should *not* be writing.

While the specific expectations change over time, we are still likely to run up against any number of societal norms when we try to live authentic lives and love in authentic ways. I expect that many interracial and same-sex couples can relate deeply to the plight of these lovers in Song of Songs. It has been within living memory that both interracial and same-sex marriages were illegal in North America; even though laws have changed, heavy stigmas against these relationships remain in many places in North America and around the world.

The reality, of course, is that none of our relationships—including the relationship of being contentedly single—can live up to all the expectations put on them. We can't possibly meet all the explicit and implicit standards for romantic love set out by our family members, friends, religious institutions, pop songs, and Hollywood movies. I, for example, am not young enough or skinny enough to be a romantic lead, and my husband and I do not kiss passionately in the rain nearly often enough for our marriage to be rom-com-worthy.

It is easy to let societal expectations damage our relationships. We might criticize the other person for not meeting some impossible, arbitrary standard. Or we might start feeling that we ourselves are unworthy to have a relationship because we do not meet some abstract criteria for a romantic love interest. But the lovers of Song of Songs show us another way—the wilderness way. Rather than let other people destroy their relationship, they find ways to separate themselves from the expectations of others and enjoy the love they share together. The wilderness allows them to have pleasure without shame, to love their own body and the body of the other, to embrace passion and to claim love.

Many religious folks try to make this book of poetry into some kind of spiritual allegory, a statement about the love of God for the people or of Christ for the church. And while I do indeed think that God loves us and that Christ loves the church, I also think that these poems are about human love, passion, and sex. And I think their presence within our sacred text is a gift for us as we struggle to learn how to live and love as humans in the world.

CONNECT

Write a love letter to someone.

CONSIDER

As we are on this Lenten journey, we realize that the love that God calls us to is different from many of the worldly messages we receive about love. What helpful and unhelpful messages do movies and TV shows send about romantic love? What positive and negative examples of love can you think of from popular culture?

SATURDAY
EXILED WOMEN LOVE THEIR CHILDREN

READ

Jeremiah 31:10–17

REFLECT

In the First Testament, the Israelites have two significant wilderness experiences. The first involves forty years of wandering in the wilderness after they escape Egypt. The second is the Babylonian exile, which is the context for the book of Jeremiah. Between 597 and 582 BCE, the Babylonians conquered Israel, destroyed the capital city of Jerusalem—including the temple—and forcibly removed many Israelites to Babylon. The prophet Jeremiah speaks to the people in the context of this exile.

While people of all genders experience the devastation of conquest and displacement, the poet here highlights the grief experienced by Rachel, who serves to represent all mothers. The women of the Babylonian exile face two great losses—they lose their homes and they lose their children. The two are intricately connected, and the grief of these losses is almost too much to bear. We hear "lamentation and bitter weeping" from the women who refuse to be comforted (v. 15).

At its heart, the message of Jeremiah is one of hope and redemption. Still, we are invited to sit with the wailing women for a while and join in their lament. As we walk with "women who love" this week, it is important to note this heartbreaking side of love: the deeper we love, the deeper we grieve. While much about the biblical world feels distant and unfamiliar, the feeling of love for our homeland and our people is timeless. And acts of violence that destroy beloved places and people are ever-present in our world. This love-soaked grief carries across the centuries to resonate in our hearts today.

When we see those we love carrying grief, our impulse is generally to step in and comfort them. Indeed, much of today's scripture reading is about God comforting the people who experience the grief of exile. Yet Rachel refuses to be comforted. It seems that comfort is something someone would welcome and seek, but perhaps there are times when we should resist comfort; times to sit with our grief; times to embrace the lost practice of lament. Can one be comforted when they lose their home? When their child dies? Should they be comforted? Eventually, of course, the wailing will subside and we can let comfort in. But perhaps not right away.

I wonder whether the urge to comfort those in deep grief isn't more about our own need for comfort than our desire to comfort others. It is not easy to sit with people in their pain; it is not easy, and it is not comfortable. If we acknowledge their grief, we might also have to acknowledge our own grief. But I'm afraid that if we deny the grief, we might also be dismissing the love. Our willingness to be uncomfortable with people before we offer them comfort may be one of the most powerful ways we can show love to each other.

In the end, the voice of God gives true comfort by sharing the good news that the mothers and their children will return to their homeland. There is hope on the other side of lament. Just as there is a time for wailing and weeping, there is also a time for singing and dancing.

The prophet says that these people who have been living in the wilderness of exile will be restored to their homes. This restoration will not be a return to the exact situation that was taken from them, but it will be a restoration to their sense of home and family. "Their life shall become like a watered garden" (v. 12)—the opposite of a barren wilderness. Just as love manifests as grief in times of loss, the mothers' deep love for their homeland and their children will spring forth as great joy when home and family are restored. Just as we should allow ourselves and others space to grieve, we are also invited to embrace the joy that flows from love.

CONNECT

Make a list of mothering people who are lamenting and weeping today; this list can include specific names and groups of people. Lift these dear ones up in prayer.

CONSIDER

The grief inherent in the Lenten season is ultimately a positive emotion. When have you experienced grief because of your love? When has love led you to joy?

Blessing for the Fifth Sunday of Lent: Women Who Love

I think you will find that the wilderness is full of lovers.
We have been sent here by circumstance.
We have fled here for freedom.
We have come to be alone.
We have come to find each other.
Why are you here, dear lover? Dear beloved?

Whatever your reasons, we are glad you have come.
We invite you into this space with all of who you are:
 your body, with its pain and its pleasure
 your heart, with its passion and its longing
 your feelings of relief and grief, anger and elation.

Our love for ourselves and for each other
 will draw us more deeply into God's love for us
 and show us the flower-strewn path through the wilderness.

So walk boldly, our dear one,
through this barren landscape—
this beautiful and beckoning wilderness.
May you find a new home as you leave an old.
May you find gratitude for deep love in the strength of your grief.
May you find your life as you lose it.
May you find pleasure in all the senses of your body.
May you find each other.
And, together, may we find the way.
Amen.

WHEN A STRANGER
—
Women Who Encounter Jesus

WEEK 6 • MONDAY

MONDAY
A SAMARITAN WOMAN TALKS TO JESUS

READ

John 4:1–26

REFLECT

When I taught college courses, I required my students to attend a certain number of campus lectures and submit reports about them. One student's report read, "I could tell the guy giving the lecture was really smart because I didn't understand a word he said." This, of course, is flawed logic, but the Samaritan woman could have easily slipped into this attitude. Her report on the Jesus lecture might have read, "I could tell the guy by the well was really spiritual because I didn't understand a word he said."

Thankfully, that's not how the Samaritan woman approaches her conversation with Jesus. Instead of deferring to him, she pushes him and questions him and ends up having what is the longest recorded conversation anyone has with Jesus in the entire Bible. She does not agree with Jesus just because he is a man with status who says things that make no sense to her. She speaks her mind and stands her ground.

When Jesus asks for a drink, the easiest and politest thing for the woman to do would have been to simply give him the drink and go on her way, but instead she challenges him from the beginning: How dare *you* ask *me* for a drink! When Jesus makes a cryptic comment about giving her living water, the easiest and politest thing for her to do would have been to smile and nod, but instead she explains to him why he cannot draw water—you don't have a bucket!—and asks him to explain himself. She goes on to ask a rhetorical and mocking question: Are you greater than our ancestor Jacob? (The answer, in her mind, is obviously no.)

Finally, the woman asks for this so-called living water. Jesus *says* he has access to living water, so she wants him to prove it. Her request may be

126

sincere, or it may be a test. It's difficult to read tone across two millennia, but I can certainly imagine many of her comments in an exasperated, challenging, snarky voice.

For example, when she says, "Sir, I see that you are a prophet" (v. 19), did she really see that Jesus was a prophet? Or was she making fun of him for trying to show off by spouting facts about her life that were quite likely public knowledge? Chances are that if a woman in a small religious community has been married that many times and is living with someone to whom she is not married, people know about it. Would she really have been impressed that someone knew her history?

After Jesus brings up her unconventional relationship situation, the woman dives right into another uncomfortable conversation—their religious difference, disagreement, and history. She says to Jesus, "Our ancestors worshiped on this mountain" (v. 20). Notice the past tense? The Samaritans didn't worship on Mount Gerizim anymore, because the Jews had destroyed the Samaritan temple. It was an ugly and uncomfortable history between the Samaritans and the Jews. Rather than politely avoid the conflicts, this woman highlights them.

Jesus responds to her comment by going into a whole speech about worshiping "in spirit and truth" (v. 24). Just like the "living water" thing, this sounds good on the surface. She could have just smiled and nodded. But instead, she thinks about it and realizes that she doesn't know what he's talking about. He's using words that sound good but don't really mean anything—at least not to her. So in verse 25 she says, essentially, "Well, when the Messiah comes, he will explain everything." Like, "Whatever. I'll wait and ask someone who knows."

And this is when Jesus says it. Whether out of love or exasperation we can't tell. Whether he had planned to say it to her right there by the well or whether he was simply pushed to say it by her refusal to accept his cryptic platitudes, we don't know. But when she says, "When the Messiah comes," Jesus responds, "I am he, the one who is speaking to you" (v. 26). Though others have said it *about* him, this is the first time in John's gospel that Jesus tells someone directly that he is the Messiah. A woman is the first person to hear Jesus' own messianic proclamation.

I am in awe of the confidence it takes for this Samaritan woman to have a serious theological conversation with a Jewish rabbi; to challenge and question him when it would have been so much easier to smile and nod and go back to her not-husband with a full jug of water. I wonder what it would take for us to have these kinds of conversations with Jesus—and with each other.

CONNECT

Have a conversation of substance with someone, perhaps at a contemporary "well" such as a coffee shop or bar.

CONSIDER

The wilderness is a place for brave conversations. When have you asked challenging questions? When have you avoided uncomfortable communication? How do you know if it is better to engage in conflict or walk away?

TUESDAY
A SAMARITAN WOMAN TELLS HER COMMUNITY ABOUT JESUS

READ

John 4:27–42

REFLECT

The woman whom Jesus meets at the well is considered by many to be the first evangelist; she goes to her community and tells them about Jesus. Kind of. It's really more of a question than a statement, more invitation than proselytization. She says, "Come and see a man who told me everything I have ever done! He cannot be the Messiah, can he?" (v. 29). She certainly seems excited, but not necessarily convinced. She is not so much trying to explain something she has already figured out as inviting people into the questions she is wrestling with. She presents the opportunity for a *relationship with* Jesus rather than insisting they commit to a particular set of *beliefs about* him.

We are told that "many Samaritans from that city believed in [Jesus] because of the woman's testimony" (v. 39). It is important to take a step back here and consider the concept of believing. Variations of the word *believe* appear all over the gospel of John—the word is used more than twice as much in John as in the other three gospels combined. When we look at this story of the woman at the well alongside the other places where John uses the term, it becomes clear that while *believe* holds a range of meaning in the gospel, it does not quite mean what we so often mean by it today. In John's gospel, for people to *believe* does not mean that they have a firm intellectual commitment to a particular concept.

For the woman at the well, belief is connected to curiosity; *belief* suggests her willingness to engage rather than avoid unusual and uncomfortable situations. There are many points at which she could have simply gone along to get along with Jesus and plenty of points where she could have exited the situation. But she doesn't. She stays and engages. She seems to have a real curiosity about who Jesus is and what he's doing and what he has to say for himself and his people. I deeply admire this kind of curiosity. When I have been privileged to talk with people who have a deep and abiding faith, I am often struck by their openness and willingness to question their church, the Bible, and even God. Questions are often viewed as hostile, but they can be indications of investment and curiosity—of belief.

In the story of the woman at the well, belief also seems to be connected to *presence*. Jesus is present with the woman, she remains present with him, and the people of the town invite Jesus to be present with them. Belief is not something that magically appears; it develops and grows as people spend time together and as they spend time with God. And the conversation—both the speaking and listening—is part of the presence. Simply inhabiting the same space is not enough. There must be an openness to both listen to and share with the other person. This is connected to another word featured in John's gospel: *abide* (see John 15:4–10). We are called to abide in Christ—to be present with Jesus and to accept his presence with us. This is part of our belief.

Another aspect of belief for the woman at the well is a willingness to prioritize Jesus. She goes to the well to get water, but after encountering Jesus with openness and curiosity, her priorities shift. She ends up leaving her water jar at the well as she goes back into the town to tell people about Jesus. Her *belief* in Jesus is not just about thoughts she thinks or words she says; her belief changes her priorities in life and affects her actions.

In contemporary evangelical culture, there tends to be a lot of talk about accepting Jesus as your "personal Savior" and a lot of people clinging to their "personal beliefs." But in this story the point of belief is not personal—belief is something the whole community explores together. The woman's first instinct as she is developing her own belief in Jesus is to share with the other people in her town. She goes to them; she asks them what they think. People's belief is tested and strengthened in community.

Ultimately, for John, belief is about *relationship*. It is not a list of thoughts you have to think. It is a living relationship you get to enter in to, a relationship that invites questions, allows vulnerability, and calls us to be present; a relationship that expects change and thrives in community. Any form of belief that falls short of this ideal will fail to provide the living water we seek on our wilderness journey.

CONNECT

Close your eyes and take a few deep breaths. Imagine yourself in a wilderness place with Jesus. What questions do you have for him? What might his answers be?

CONSIDER

During this Lenten journey, how are you seeking to nurture a relationship with Jesus? How will you continue to nurture your relationship beyond the season of Lent?

WEDNESDAY
A WOMAN RECEIVES GRACE

READ

John 8:1–11

REFLECT

The key character in this story, like so many women in Scripture, is not named by the author. She is generally referred to as "the woman caught in the act of adultery." In addition to being a clunky moniker, this identification hardly seems fair to the woman whom the religious leaders unjustly drag in front of a crowd. She was not formally found guilty of or condemned for committing adultery in the first century, so why should we stick her with that charge in the twenty-first century? And even if she was, in fact, guilty of adultery, nobody deserves to be defined by one poor choice. If we knew this woman's whole story, I imagine there are other names we could give her: the woman who loved her children; the woman with a beautiful voice; the woman who was wounded.

The truth is that we don't know her history. We don't know what her relationship was with the man she was found with or with the men who dragged her before Jesus. Was she just a random woman chosen as a prop to try to trick Jesus? Did one of the scribes have a grudge against her? Was the man she was with a Pharisee whose life would be easier if she were out of the picture?

We do know that this interaction the woman has with the religious authorities would have been traumatic. How consensual was this sexual encounter? If she was indeed "caught in the act," we can assume she was wearing little to no clothes when she was grabbed by a group of men and forced to stand in front of an even larger group of men all with the threat of execution by stoning hanging over her. When the men ask Jesus what they should do, does she have any idea who Jesus is or how he might respond?

I am glad, certainly, that the woman survives this ordeal; that the men put down their stones and go away. I also wonder how she feels. Relief, yes. But where is she supposed to go now? Will her husband or father take her back into the home after this public shaming? Can she even return to "the scene of the crime" to get her clothes? What will her life possibly be like in the community after this event?

Most biblical scholars agree that this story did not appear in the earliest versions of John's gospel. It was added later, which leads me to two questions: Why was it added? And why was it allowed to stay? From a narrative perspective, this story furthers our understanding of how desperate the religious leaders are to trap Jesus. From a theological and ethical perspective, there are certainly important lessons here about grace and forgiveness, about justice and integrity. Perhaps some of these considerations were at play when the powers that be decided to include this extraneous segment in the gospel of John.

Whatever the reason for its inclusion, I am grateful that the story of this woman who received grace is part of our sacred text because it lets us think about grace particularly in the context of our bodies. As in the first century, we still live in a society that tends to elevate certain sexual sins above other sins—and to define as sin many sexual acts and attitudes that are not, in fact, sinful. Still today, women, transgender people, nonbinary people, and men who are seen as "too feminine" are more likely to be shamed and punished for perceived sexual sins than cisgender and heterosexual men.

Ironically, this story of Jesus offering grace to a woman the community seeks to shame is often used in the church today to silence survivors of sexualized violence. Religious leaders sometimes liken the perpetrator of abuse (most often a man) to the woman caught in adultery. We are all sinners, they say, and we therefore must forgive any sin that has been committed and must not expect any form of accountability. But this kind of reckless forgiveness and cheap grace is not what Jesus offers here. Protection for powerful abusers is not what Jesus is going for. The *man*, who was most certainly also caught in the act of adultery, is not brought before the crowd.

This is a story of grace for one on the margins, for one who is a victim (in one way or another) of a patriarchal system. I don't know how Jesus would have responded to the man, but he does not condemn this woman who was caught in the act of adultery. He is not impressed or titillated or scandalized by her actions. He gets rid of her abusers and then sends her on her way. We don't know what happened next, but I hope she received the same grace from others that she received from Jesus. I hope she was able to extend that grace to herself.

CONNECT

Sing or listen to "Amazing Grace"—or another song that expresses the deep grace offered by Jesus.

CONSIDER

Share about a time when you felt shame. If you experienced grace, what did that look like? If you did not, what would it have looked like to receive grace? What would it look like now to receive God's grace and release your shame?

THURSDAY
A WOMAN SEEKS HEALING

READ

Mark 5:21–34

REFLECT

Like the woman at the well and the woman caught in adultery, the woman in this story is also known by her circumstance rather than her name: the woman with a flow of blood. Of course, the vast majority of women have a "flow of blood" periodically for decades of their lives, so it's not a very specific identifier. But for this particular woman, her blood has been flowing nonstop for twelve years. In addition to the physical discomfort, the hygiene issues, and the utter inconvenience of the situation, this woman's illness also means that she has been living in a state of ritual impurity for twelve years. Her ability to participate in religious practices and interact with other people is severely limited. She is physically sick and socially isolated—definitely a woman in the wilderness, looking for direction, desperate to find relief.

Because of her desperation and, Jesus indicates, her faith, she reaches out to Jesus and touches the hem of his cloak. It is a bold move, and I love this woman's willingness to seek what she needs for herself, even when it means imposing on others.

Jesus is on his way to do something most would consider more important than healing a random woman on the street. He is on his way to heal someone who is arguably more important than this woman—the daughter of a synagogue leader—and more critically ill. Jairus's daughter is "at the point of death" (v. 23) while the woman's condition, though miserable, does not seem to be life-threatening. Yet the woman interrupts Jesus' journey toward Jairus's daughter in order to seek healing for herself. She imposes herself on Jesus when he is busy doing something important. She also imposes herself by daring to touch Jesus' clothes. This might seem like a small thing, but because she is ritually impure, her touch will make Jesus ritually impure as well.

I cannot imagine myself in this woman's position. I *hate* to impose on others. I never want to be a bother. I don't want to feel like I'm in the way or asking something of someone that they'd rather not give. My hunch is that women have been particularly conditioned to avoid imposing on others, and especially on men.

And it's not only that we don't want to impose, but also that we have a very broad understanding of what might be an imposition. We expect people to be upset when we ask something of them; we expect them to be irritated, resentful, even angry. And sometimes they might be, which is okay. But often we aren't imposing as much as we think. Where, really, is the line between imposition and interaction? People often like to be acknowledged, to be asked, to be valued.

Jesus certainly doesn't condemn the woman for being an imposition. If he were concerned about the delay in getting to Jairus's daughter, Jesus could just keep walking. The woman has touched his cloak and is already healed. He could have felt her touch, been irritated, and kept going to his "more important" task. But he doesn't keep walking. He stops and asks who has touched him. He gives the woman even more time and energy than she has asked of him, even more than she really needs.

The narrator says that the woman tells Jesus "the whole truth" (v. 33). We often think this is an imposition, too, don't we? To share the fullness of our stories, to burden people with the sad realities of our lives. I don't know exactly what she tells Jesus; it's possible that "the whole truth" takes a while to tell—yet another imposition. But Jesus gladly listens. He then calls her "daughter" and sends her away healed and in peace.

We can learn from both the woman's willingness to impose herself on Jesus and from Jesus' gracious response to her reaching out. Indeed, human interaction is not an imposition; it is what we are here for.

CONNECT

Trace your hand on a piece of paper. Inside the hand, write about the wilderness you are in and the healing you would like to experience; this might be physical, spiritual, mental, or relational healing. Then, around the outside of your hand, write Jesus' words to the woman: "Daughter [or son or my child], your faith has made you well; go in peace, and be healed" (Mark 5:34). Write these words several times and let them sink into your spirit. Place your hand inside the traced hand and invite the healing presence of the Holy Spirit.

CONSIDER

Is there a situation right now where you might need to impose in order to get the help you need for yourself or someone else? Is there something you can do to allow those who might come to you for help to feel less like they are imposing on you?

FRIDAY
JOANNA AND SUSANNA SUPPORT JESUS

READ

Luke 8:1–3

REFLECT

When we think of Jesus' disciples, twelve men generally come to mind. But we know that many more than twelve people believed in Jesus and traveled with him on his journeys. The gospel of Luke identifies some of those people as women, and the women named here are not just casual hangers-on; they are an integral part of Jesus' ministry.

Mary Magdalene is probably the best known of Jesus' female followers, and we will look more closely at her in the reflections after Easter. Joanna and Susanna, on the other hand, are probably not familiar to most people. I was named after Joanna, which is the only reason I have been aware of Joanna and Susanna's presence in Scripture. These two don't get a lot of ink. Joanna shows up only here and in Luke 24:10, among the women announcing the resurrection. Susanna is named only here, but I imagine she was present at the resurrection and other times when "and others" are mentioned.

Even though this is a brief passage, it provides some significant information about these two women. We know that they have both "been cured of evil spirits and infirmities" (8:2). This, of course, is a vague description, and it's unclear exactly what the women have suffered from in the past. Without knowing the details, we can still understand that their commitment to Jesus is related to personal experiences of healing; in some way their lives are better now because of Jesus, so they have chosen to follow him. On the one hand, it would be nice to know more details, to know exactly what infirmities Joanna and Susanna had experienced. But on the other hand, the vagueness allows us to more easily put ourselves in their place. Whatever you have experienced might be what one of these women had experienced. Jesus' healing covers many, many situations.

When James, John, and Simon Peter witnessed the power of Jesus, "they left everything and followed him" (5:11). This seems to be what Mary, Joanna, Susanna, and "many other" women have done as well. While not explicitly named among the twelve apostles, these women are part of Jesus' inner circle, traveling with him from town to town just like "the twelve."

Not only do these women follow Jesus, but they also minister to him "out of their own resources" (8:3). Joanna and Susanna were likely women of some status and wealth, giving them the freedom to be absent from their households and the ability to contribute financially to the Jesus movement. It is interesting to consider what the social dynamics of Jesus' group were like, as it seems that most of the men were of lower social standing than the women. Did some of the men object to women being among them? Did Joanna, accustomed to living in Herod's household, complain about the hard ground and the unkempt fishermen?

Joanna's connection to Herod's household is notable not only because of the social and economic status it suggests but also because of the conflicts between Herod and Jesus. This is the same Herod who had Jesus' cousin John the Baptist beheaded; the same Herod who will participate in the events that lead to Jesus' crucifixion. And, apparently, the same Herod who inadvertently helps fund Jesus' ministry through the wife of one of his employees. I imagine that Joanna's presence with Jesus' entourage could have been a challenge for them both. Joanna had to be willing to risk her relationships within Herod's household to be part of Jesus' ministry. And Jesus had to be willing to trust someone with ties to an enemy and to be willing to accept money from a disreputable source.

Susana and Joanna offer us deep lessons of generosity in the wilderness. They are generous with their financial resources, to be sure. They are also generous with their time, with their relationships, with their lives. Their generosity is not based in obligation or shame but grows *in response to* the healing that Jesus offers. As we follow, learn from, and are healed by Jesus, may we also respond with bold generosity.

CONNECT

Almsgiving is another common Lenten practice. Give of your resources (time or money) to a ministry that is doing God's work in the world.

CONSIDER

How do you imagine the different people traveling with Jesus got along with each other? How might the dynamics in that group have been similar to what you've experienced in your church or other groups?

SATURDAY
A CANAANITE WOMAN CHALLENGES JESUS

READ

Matthew 15:21–28

REFLECT

When I was in seminary, one of my beloved (male) professors thought it would be "fun" for me to take a class at the nearby Southern Baptist seminary. "Fun for *you* to hear my horror stories," I replied. I had absolutely no desire to go into a space where I knew I was not wanted; where I would find myself at the mercy of men who thought they were better than me.

Which is why I have deep admiration for this Canaanite woman who presents herself to Jesus and insists on what she needs until she gets it. Just like the woman with the flow of blood, this woman is not afraid to be an imposition. While the first woman disrupts Jesus for her own healing, the Canaanite woman imposes on Jesus for the sake of her daughter.

This woman is not deterred when Jesus ignores her. I suppose this is understandable. Some people don't readily pick up on social cues. Being ignored isn't necessarily hostile; it could be that the person just doesn't notice you, right?

And she is not deterred when the disciples tell Jesus (surely loud enough for her to hear them) to send her away. This is a little harder to ignore, but she's not there for the disciples. These are the guys who wanted Jesus to send all the children away (Luke 18:15) and told him to send the crowds away (Matthew 14:15). It's kind of their thing to tell Jesus to send people away. Then Jesus' thing is to say, "No way! They can stay!" Except that's not what happens here. Jesus doesn't say she can stay. He says that he is not there for her kind. He calls her a dog (15:26).

And still, amazingly, she is not deterred. We can certainly apply the contemporary feminist rallying cry to this ancient woman: Nevertheless, she persisted. She persisted through neglect, dismissal, and outright hostility.

141

Back in my seminary days, just the thought of people wanting me to go away, the thought of them thinking they were superior and calling me names (probably behind my back) was enough to keep me in my place—out of the Southern Baptist seminary. But this woman is willing to endure contempt and insults as she seeks healing for her daughter.

I admire her immensely, and I am curious about how she can enter into such an uncomfortable situation, why she is willing to be such an imposition and endure such treatment. The primary reason, I expect, is sheer maternal desperation. Her daughter is being *tormented*. She will do anything it takes to bring relief to her daughter. Her own comfort—even her own life—is not important compared to the prospect of ending her daughter's pain.

The second reason I expect that the woman can face this hostility is the reason that Jesus gives for finally healing her daughter: she has great faith. Faith in Jesus' power to heal, yes, of course. If she didn't truly believe that Jesus could heal her daughter, she wouldn't be there shouting in a crowd and absorbing insults. She has faith in Jesus' miraculous abilities. But she also, I think, has faith in Jesus' humanity. He ignores her. He insults her. But she knows that he actually has a compassionate heart; that he really does care about her and her daughter. She has faith that, in the end, Jesus will treat her with love and respect.

The mother seems to pull Jesus into his more compassionate self by sheer force of will. This strategy reminds me of challenging times as a parent: waiting pleasantly and patiently (on the outside, at least) for a child to stop calling me names and throwing things so we could discuss the issue at hand. Because so many times the negligence, the dismissal, the hostility is not about you, it's about all the other things that person is dealing with. So many times compassion will win out if we give it just a little time, just a little space to emerge.

In the wilderness we will encounter many types of people in many different challenging situations. Can we have faith in other people to, eventually, do the right thing? Can we remain calm and give them encouragement and space to act out of compassion? There is something wonderful and powerful about this woman who lives with such fierce faith in both Jesus' divinity and his humanity.

CONNECT

The wilderness is a place of desperation. If you were to fall down at Jesus' feet, what would you ask for? How might Jesus respond?

CONSIDER

When have you been in a situation similar to that of the Canaanite woman, where you were disrespected? How did you respond? When have you been in a situation similar to that of the disciples and Jesus, where you tried to dismiss people who were bothering you? What (could have) pulled you toward compassion?

Blessing for Palm Sunday: From Women Who Encounter Jesus

We have all been searching in the wilderness:
    for healing of our bodies and spirits, healing of ourselves and those we
        love;
    for compassion and community, for traveling companions;
    for guidance and answers, or at least for more faithful questions.

In our searching we have found Jesus:
    even though his followers tried to push us away
    even though some said he had more important people to tend
    even though we didn't know we were looking for him.

In our searching we have found ourselves:
    our passions and our voices
    our wellness and our worth
    our integrity and our generosity.

In our searching we have found a blessing.
Let these words accompany you as they have accompanied us
    in the many kinds of wilderness we traverse:

    Your need is not burden.
    Your presence is not imposition.
    Your body is not shameful.
    Your voice is not too loud.

    For the sake of healing—your own and the world's—
    you are allowed to interrupt and insist,
    to challenge and question,
    to give and receive with generosity and grace.
    In the wildness of the wilderness,
    where conflict and companionship
    draw us into faith,
    may your faith make you well
    and may you go in peace.
    Amen.

HOLY WEEK

HIS PRECIOUS BLOOD
—
Women Who Tend to Jesus' Death

The scripture readings and reflections for Holy Week are intentionally brief to allow more space for contemplation. Perhaps you want to read through the suggested scriptures more than once. Maybe you will enter a time of silent meditation before or after reading the reflection. Or you may want to sink more deeply into the Connect and Consider suggestions. As we approach the foot of the cross, I invite you to slow down, rest, and breathe.

HOLY MONDAY
MARY ANOINTS JESUS

READ

John 12:1–8

REFLECT

With this extravagant gesture, Mary of Bethany demonstrates her love of Jesus and her knowledge of his imminent death. The intimacy of this act is staggering. The palpable grief of this scene is heartbreaking.

Mary is surely not the only person in the room who has heard Jesus talk about his upcoming death, who has heard the many voices condemning Jesus and felt the tension in the air. Mary should not be the only one besides Jesus to anticipate what this week will hold, but it seems that she is. Maybe the others are just not as perceptive as she is. Or maybe they refuse to allow themselves to see the signs because they can't bear the thought of Jesus' death. Whatever the reason, only Mary uses these embalming spices on Jesus' body; only Mary kneels and wipes Jesus' feet with her hair; only Mary disregards propriety to acknowledge the danger and grief that is closing in around them all.

Her act of love and acknowledgment must have been a deep gift to Jesus. He could see in her teary eyes that she shared his sorrow. He could smell in the fragrant perfume that she understood he would die. He could feel in the touch of her fingers that she loved him deeply.

As he sits with his friends around the dinner table, I imagine Jesus experiences the particular kind of aching loneliness that comes from feeling isolated in a crowd. Jesus is surrounded by people who love him and supposedly know him, yet nobody is really sitting with him in the horror of his reality. No one shares his dread or his grief—until Mary walks in. She kneels. She breaks open the jar of perfume. And suddenly Jesus has a companion in the wilderness. Suddenly he knows that at least one person is willing—and able—to walk with him toward the cross.

CONNECT

The woman who anoints Jesus' feet brings to mind the story of Jesus washing his disciples' feet on the night he is arrested. Read that story (John 13:1–20) and prayerfully wash your own feet or someone else's.

CONSIDER

When have you felt lonely? When have you felt that the people around you didn't understand what you were going through? How can you be present for others who are experiencing this kind of loneliness?

HOLY TUESDAY
FEMALE SERVANTS IDENTIFY PETER

READ

Matthew 26:69–75

REFLECT

We usually consider this story from Peter's perspective—his despair, his fear, his shame. But what of the women who identify Peter as a follower of Jesus? Their identity as "servants" does not tell us much about the specific roles they play in the high priest's household. Perhaps they are cleaning or working security detail. Maybe they are on their way to the kitchen or gathering laundry. Maybe they have just finished their shift for the night and are heading home.

I wonder whether these women are aware of what is happening inside with Jesus and Caiaphas: the harsh interrogation, the false accusations, the physical abuse. Have they picked up on the tension and fear surrounding this wonder-working rabbi, Jesus? Did they overhear confidential priestly conversations—co-conspirators whispering in corners, raised voices behind closed doors? Were they unwilling witnesses to all the plotting and scheming about why Jesus must die and how it would happen?

These women must have some knowledge of Jesus, some kind of connection, some care or at least curiosity, because they recognize Peter: "You also were with Jesus" (v. 69). Neither of the women *ask* Peter about his relationship with Jesus; their statements are ones of simple fact. Do they realize the effect their statements will have on Peter? Do they anticipate his fear? Have they underestimated how much they put him in danger? And when they see the panic in his eyes, are they thrilled to realize their power or ashamed at their thoughtless pronouncement?

We have all been there, haven't we?

We've tried to keep our heads down, do our jobs. We've chosen to not pay too much attention, to not draw the obvious conclusions. Sometimes evil is happening on the other side of the wall and we aren't part of it. Except to ignore it. And maybe to cook food for the people perpetrating it.

We've said the obvious thing without regard for the power of our words. We've been so caught up in our own small reality that we fail to think through how we might be affecting the lives of those around us.

For our moments in the courtyard, whether we are in the place of Peter or the women servants, God have mercy.

CONNECT

Pay attention today. Who do you see? What are they doing? What are they saying? What is happening in the spaces around you? What kind of wilderness are others experiencing?

CONSIDER

What is our responsibility in situations where we know of, but are not actively participating in, harmful activities? Can you think of times when you have ignored things that others were doing? Can you think of times you tried to intervene?

HOLY WEDNESDAY
PILATE'S WIFE WARNS HER HUSBAND

READ

Matthew 27:15–26

REFLECT

Pilate's wife joins the company of Lot's wife and Job's wife—unnamed women whose suffering is presented as a minor footnote in their husbands' stories. But unlike these other wives, Pilate's wife exercises power and has a voice.

She has the power to "send word"; people are available to do and say what she tells them. She has the power to interrupt the work of her husband, the governor. And she expects that she might even have the power to influence his political decisions.

She also, surprisingly, claims a power of spiritual insight, relating information that came to her in a dream. The Bible establishes a clear pattern of God speaking to people in dreams. At least thirteen people in Scripture receive messages from God through their dreams; among them are Laban, Joseph, Jacob, Daniel, Abimelech, Solomon, Joseph (Mary's husband), and even Nebuchadnezzar and Pharaoh. Pilate's wife is the only woman in Scripture whose dream we get to hear about; she is also the only non-Jewish person apparently able to interpret her own dream.

While her dream is a form of spiritual power, it also causes her to suffer "a great deal" (v. 19). She does, indeed, experience a particular kind of suffering: she sees something terrible coming and is not able to stop it. Her suffering also comes from the fact that she has enough power to make her think she *might* be able to stop the tragedy she sees coming. But in the end, it turns out that she is not quite powerful enough. Which is excruciating.

This is the only time that Pilate's wife is mentioned in Scripture. I wonder about the rest of her story. Did she decide to plead her case with Pilate in person, only to realize it was too late? Did she watch the crucifixion in horror? Did she stand with the women at the foot of the cross? Or did she shrug her shoulders and move on, determined to enjoy her life and ignore her dreams?

CONNECT

If you have a dream journal, read through the last month or so. If not, write down any dreams you have (and remember) this week. At the end of the week, prayerfully read through the dreams and consider whether there is something God might be saying through them.

CONSIDER

Think about a situation where you had some power but were unable to effect the hoped-for outcome. How did you feel? Is there anything you would do differently if faced with a similar situation?

MAUNDY THURSDAY
WOMEN WEEP FOR JESUS

READ

Luke 23:26–31

REFLECT

It's possible that the women mentioned in today's passage were being paid to wail and beat their chests. In the ancient Roman world, professional mourning was a role filled almost exclusively by women who were hired to add drama and prestige to funerals and, in this case, executions.

Whether or not these women were paid to lament Jesus' walk to the cross, they appear in the story as anonymous observers. We do not know what, if any, connection they have to Jesus. It is possible that their wailing is not a protest against Jesus' death specifically, but a protest against the system of state-sanctioned execution in general.

Crucifixion was a uniquely Roman form of murder, and a blatantly public one. The intent of crucifixion was not only to punish and eliminate people who were perceived as threats to the empire, but also to serve as a highly visible warning for others who might consider stepping out of line. That's why Jesus and the others being crucified had to carry the beams of their crosses to the posts that stood at the top of the hill—so everyone could witness their suffering and humiliation.

Even if these women do not know Jesus, they know the system, and they weep for those who fall victim to it. In this context, their public mourning becomes prophetic witness; beating our breasts can be a protest against violence. We need people who are willing to grieve the general state of a society that operates through violence. We need people to wail for everyone who is caught up in the oppressive system of empire—friend and stranger alike.

Jesus tells the women, "Daughters of Jerusalem, do not weep for me, but weep for yourselves and for your children" (v. 28). And perhaps that is what they are doing. Perhaps in Jesus' tortured body they see the bodies of their own sons, oppressed and at the mercy of the state. Perhaps their own fathers, brothers, cousins, have been harassed and abused by law enforcement and punished, even killed, by soldiers who looked very much like those forcing Jesus up the hill. Perhaps this is not their first time processing to the place of The Skull. It likely won't be their last.

It turns out there is not such a clear line between personal and public grief, between individual and social sorrow. Our heartbreak over one person's crucifixion is heartbreak over the system of state oppression and execution. Our wailing in response to one act of violence is wailing against the cycles of violence we see repeated over and over again. These women's cries as they follow behind Jesus echo in our hearts today as we lament the patterns of oppression and abuse that continue to persist in our world.

CONNECT

What personal grief are you carrying through the wilderness? What strangers do you grieve for? Offer all this grief to God in prayer.

CONSIDER

What current societal practices should cause us to wail and beat our breasts? How can you engage in lament as an important Lenten spiritual practice?

GOOD FRIDAY
MARY MOURNS HER SON

READ

John 19:25b–27

REFLECT

The women stand there, near the cross, where they can see the marks of torture on Jesus' body. Where they can hear his gasps for air and his insistent words. The male disciples—except for "the disciple whom [Jesus] loved" (v. 26)—are conspicuously absent.

There are, of course, political reasons to disappear when Jesus is crucified. Those seen near Jesus' cross would become known as disciples of the condemned rabbi and part of his ragtag religious movement. As Peter's denial suggests, there was real risk involved in being associated with Jesus.

There are also significant emotional reasons to wander away from Jesus when things get ugly. It is really hard to be near someone you love when they are in pain. Watching your child suffer, as Jesus' mother does, is excruciating. For everyone who loves Jesus, it would be both politically safer and emotionally easier to keep their distance from the foot of the cross.

It is no different today. If we stay near those who are condemned, marginalized, and exploited by the powers that be, we risk being condemned, marginalized, and exploited ourselves. When we move closer to our loved ones in their times of pain and struggle, we risk grief and broken hearts.

Despite the political and emotional risks, the women and the beloved disciple stay near Jesus. And we see something amazing: community forms at the foot of the cross. The women and the disciple are taking this risk *together*. They are facing the pain *together*. In Jesus' words to his mother and beloved disciple, he acknowledges the bond that is formed in such shared courage and grief.

The relationship between the beloved disciple and Jesus' mother demonstrates that while there is risk involved in a life near the cross, there is also deep blessing. We find protection, support, and love among those willing to gather and look, together, at the reality of suffering.

CONNECT

Who has been with you through a difficult situation? Reach out to them in some way this week.

CONSIDER

Why do you think these women and the beloved disciple remained near the cross? Why did other disciples leave? What helps us stick with difficult situations?

HOLY SATURDAY
WOMEN BEAR WITNESS TO JESUS' DEATH

READ

Luke 23:44–56

REFLECT

In John's gospel the women stand near the cross, whereas in Luke they stand "at a distance" (v. 49). Still, they are present. They watch. And they do not return home after the crucifixion. "All of [Jesus'] acquaintances" remain after the gawking spectators have left (v. 49). They stand with their grief, their disbelief, their anger, their fear. They stay to comfort each other, to keep company with those who understand. But eventually most of them go home, too. Only "the women who had come with him from Galilee" follow Jesus' body (v. 55). Only the women—and Joseph of Arimathea—stay close enough to see the body laid in the tomb.

Why do the women stay when everyone else has gone home? Why follow the wrapped body of Jesus from the hill where he was crucified down to the rock-hewn tomb? Are they already anticipating their role in anointing the body with spices, thinking ahead and realizing that they will need to know where the body is? If so, this is some impressive forethought amid extreme grief and trauma.

Perhaps they follow Jesus less out of practical forethought and more out of emotion. Maybe they are simply not ready to let him go. They want to stay with their friend, their teacher, their son, for as long as possible. They do not go home like the others, because *Jesus is their home*. They have nowhere else to go.

The final line of today's reading stops me in my tracks: "On the Sabbath they rested according to the commandment." I am stunned that amid this intense experience, the women still practice Sabbath. I find it difficult to stop and rest in the best of times, yet somehow these women manage to stop even though there are spices to prepare and a body to anoint. They must have so much nervous energy from anxiety, fear, and grief. Yet they rest. In the resting they honor Jesus; they also honor their grief.

On this Holy Saturday, can you join the women in resting? Can you honor the sacred space of this in-between day with a slowed pace, a calm spirit, and a few deep breaths?

CONNECT

Holy Saturday often gets lost in the space between Good Friday and Easter Sunday. Let the stillness and grief of this day sink in as you sit in silent meditation for ten minutes or more.

CONSIDER

What do you think the women talked about as they followed Joseph to the tomb? As they prepared the spices? As they rested on the Sabbath? How do you tend to respond to acute grief in your own life?

Blessing for Easter Sunday:
From the Women Who Tend to Jesus' Death

We have become comfortable in the wilderness.
    That is why we were able to recognize what was coming,
        why we were willing to speak when others wished us silent,
        why we stayed when others left.
    That is how we were able to stare death in the face
        and follow the body of our beloved One to the tomb.
Because we have become comfortable in the wilderness.

And so we come to the tomb this morning
to do the wilderness work of grieving
    of anointing
    of saying goodbye.

We come to the tomb and find
    that the landscape of the wilderness has changed!
We see an opening where we expected a stone blockade.
We squint into brightness where we expected shadows.
We hear heavenly voices proclaim good news
    where we expected
    utter silence.

We come to the tomb for death and encounter
Life—
an entirely different kind of wilderness!

We have become comfortable in the wilderness, it's true,
but this is a new wilderness—
    good and holy but, somehow, maybe not as comfortable.
The wilderness of Resurrection invites us to
new curiosity
new energy
new joy
new purpose
new life.

On this Resurrection Sunday,
in this Easter season,
may your wilderness be renewed.
May you find stones rolled away.
May light flood the shadowy places.
May you hear good news where you least expect it.
And if you, like us, can't understand it all,
may you receive it anyway:
All the openness, all the joy, all the life.
Receive all that this confounding and inexplicable morning offers—
as it was ours then, it is yours now.
Amen. And thanks be.

SONGS OF LOUDEST PRAISE
—
Women Who Proclaim Jesus' Resurrection

MONDAY
MARY MAGDALENE, MARY THE MOTHER OF JAMES, AND SALOME IN MARK

READ

Mark 16:1–8

REFLECT

In this first week of the Easter season, we will explore the resurrection accounts from all four gospels—all of which feature women at the empty tomb hearing the news that Jesus is risen! In Mark's account—the oldest of the gospels—three women bring spices to the tomb early in the morning: Mary Magdalene, Mary the mother of James, and Salome. These are the same three women said to be watching the crucifixion in the previous chapter.

After the crucifixion, the two Marys take note of where Jesus' body is laid. Then, presumably, they go home to observe the Sabbath. But as soon as they can—"very early on the first day of the week" (v. 2)—they head toward the tomb, prepared to anoint Jesus' body. On the way to the tomb, they ask each other, "Who will roll away the stone?" (v. 3). This seems like something they would want to have figured out ahead of time. Maybe they should have invited some extra people—strong people—with them that morning, because this is no little rock we're talking about. The women are up early with spices packed, heading to anoint Jesus, but there is every possibility they will get there and not be able to get into the tomb.

That's how it is in the wake of grief, isn't it? We are disoriented and foggy. We want to do *something*, but we don't always have the capacity to make good choices and plan for contingencies. Grief is, indeed, a wilderness space, and the women do the only thing they know to do: they walk toward the tomb with their spices. It is too much for them to think through all the details, to plan a few steps ahead, to consider all the practicalities involved. It's just one step in front of the other, clinging to the items they will use to anoint the body of the one they love.

It turns out, of course, that they don't need to move the stone after all. It has already been rolled away. By the "young man dressed in a white robe" (v. 5)? By some invisible cosmic force? By the resurrected Jesus himself? We don't know. We only know that it is gone, and so the women go inside the tomb. Which really is a bold move. The open tomb could be a trap, with soldiers lying in wait. Or it could be inhabited by a wild animal primed to attack. Or it could simply be dank and putrid—because it's a tomb. Perhaps the women walk into the tomb because they are particularly brave. Or perhaps they are still in their grief fog, not really processing the situation, not thinking through potential dangers.

When the women do enter the tomb, they are alarmed by what they see—a guy in white sitting where they expect to see Jesus' dead body. Or maybe they are alarmed by what they don't see—Jesus' dead body. This unexpected turn of events jolts them out of their fog. They are still disoriented, but it is a hyperalert disorientation rather than a mindless one. They are keenly aware that the world is not how they expected it to be. And while that is, ultimately, good news, in the moment it is alarming, terrifying, amazing.

"Terror and amazement had seized them" (v. 8).

Mark's version of the resurrection story is not the swelling-music, "Hallelujah!," flowers-and-sunshine celebration that we have come to expect on Resurrection Sunday. Terror is not what we generally associate with Easter. Amazement might seem more appropriate, but even that is a rare experience when we hear the familiar story year after year.

Mark's narration of the event is a reminder of Easter's original intensity. It is also, I think, a gentle encouragement for us to approach the Easter celebration as our authentic selves. While the startling discovery of renewed life is an emotional experience, there are no right or wrong emotions to feel when faced with the overwhelming reality of the resurrection, when faced with the fullness of life in God's love and power. Some people are terrified. Some are amazed. Some are in a fog. Some are hyperalert. Any emotion, any response, is expected and accepted in the strange emptiness of the tomb.

Despite the instructions to "go and tell," the women "said nothing to anyone, for they were afraid" (v. 8). Alarmed, terrified, amazed, afraid. God's life in the world does not follow our rules. It is, in many ways, more disorienting than death. The resurrection is, ultimately, good news. It is *the* good news. And it is also its own kind of terrifying, amazing wilderness to navigate.

CONNECT

Like the women who went to the tomb, get up very early and watch the sunrise. Take deep breaths and relax into God's presence as you experience the wonder of a new day beginning.

CONSIDER

Think about an event or situation that brought up mixed emotions for you. What happened? How did you feel? How did you think you should feel? How did you deal with your range of feelings?

TUESDAY
MARY MAGDALENE, MARY THE MOTHER OF JAMES, JOANNA, AND "THE OTHER WOMEN" IN LUKE

READ

Luke 24:1–12

REFLECT

Once again, we encounter terrified women at the tomb. It is clearly difficult for people to wrap their heads around the whole resurrection thing. As difficult as Jesus' death was, his new life seems at least equally disorienting to these women.

This question from men in dazzling clothes resonates still today: "Why do you look for the living among the dead?" (v. 5). Because we do that sometimes, don't we? We look for things in the wrong places. We misread situations. But this question hardly seems fair to the women in this context because they are *not* looking for the living among the dead. They are looking for the dead among the dead. They have come to anoint Jesus' dead body, and this is a brave and noble thing. So often we tend to avoid death, to shy away from it; we certainly don't go *looking* for it. But here are Mary Magdalene, Joanna, Mary, and "the other women out looking for a dead body at the crack of dawn.

These women are committed to Jesus. They are also good Jewish women. For one thing, they faithfully observe the Sabbath despite their grief and trauma. And then they come to tend to the dead—an action that is considered a particularly good deed in Jewish thought, because a deed done for someone who has died is a deed done out of sheer kindness with no expectation for repayment.

The women are being as faithful as they know how, and then these gleaming strangers suggest that they are doing the wrong thing—or rather, that they are looking for the wrong thing. It still happens, you know, that faithful folks can focus so much on their faithfulness that they miss the bigger things that God is doing. We shush children so worship can go smoothly. We cut benevolence spending so we can balance the budget. We pray for peace yet fight amongst ourselves. Even all these years after the resurrection, we sometimes still forget we should be looking for the living instead of the dead.

When you serve a God who specializes in the unimaginable, it's hard to imagine what God might be up to. This makes it hard to know what, exactly, we should be looking for. Those words must have sounded so strange to the women: "[Jesus] is not here but has risen" (v. 5). The women aren't expecting this news, but they come to embrace it. While this story starts in fear, the women leave in confidence.

This shift from fear to confidence comes *after* the gleaming men tell the women, "Remember how [Jesus] told you . . ." (v. 6). In the terror of the past few days—the chaos of the arrest, the trauma of the crucifixion, the grief and stress of the Sabbath waiting—it seems they have forgotten. Forgotten Jesus' words; forgotten Jesus' promises; forgotten the all-encompassing *life* of Jesus that drew them to him in the first place. They know Jesus was special, of course they do. That's why they followed him around, supported him, loved him. They know he was extraordinary. But then he died. And the world seemed so normal again. And Jesus' body seemed like any other body.

So they go to look for the dead among the dead and are surprised to find life instead of death. They are drawn out of their grief-haze when they remember. They remember that they shouldn't be surprised. That Jesus had told them that all this would happen. They remember that they had believed Jesus when he spoke to them then, and they decide they will believe him now.

At the point of remembering, their terror shifts to confidence. Sometimes we just need to be reminded of what we know, to believe our own eyes, our own ears, our own hearts. Sometimes we just need to remember—and to remember together. In remembering, we can realize that we should be looking not for the dead, but for the living. In this Easter season and beyond, may you remember that the life of God is always present in the world and always present with us.

CONNECT

Visit a grave (or another site) to remember someone you love.

CONSIDER

Share about a time when you experienced God's faithfulness during a wilderness season. How can remembering this experience help you in any current struggles you face?

WEDNESDAY
MARY MAGDALENE AND "THE OTHER MARY" IN MATTHEW

READ

Matthew 28:1–10

REFLECT

When my father-in-law died unexpectedly, I showed up at my in-laws' house, gathered all his magazines, and started calling around to cancel the subscriptions. When my own father died, I started working on the poem he had asked me to write for his funeral. As a pastor, in the wake of death I generally help loved ones plan the memorial service. *Is the church building available? Who will play piano? What hymns will we sing?* I've got you.

When tragedy strikes, when grief is heavy, it's nice to have a concrete task, something to do that feels useful and productive. This is the case for the women of Mark's and Luke's stories who bring spices to the tomb to anoint Jesus' body. But in Matthew, as far as we can tell, the two Marys come empty-handed. They don't come to anoint the body; they come "to see the tomb" (v. 1).

I love the emptiness of their hands, the unproductiveness of their action, the fact that, in their grief, they are simply drawn back to Jesus with no clear purpose or intention. They just want to be near him again. To see. To bear witness. And the angel honors their desire when he invites them to "come, see the place where he lay" (v. 6).

The women come to see, and they witness quite a production. There is an earthquake—unique to Matthew's gospel. And they see the angel descend from heaven and roll the stone away! (In the other three gospels, the stone is already rolled away when the women arrive.) The appearance of the angel is so startling that the guards are frightened into a comatose state. The women do, indeed, see something extraordinary—and they are told to go tell the disciples that *they* will also see. As the women run to share this message, they see the most astonishing thing yet—the risen Jesus himself! They see him and touch him and hear his reassuring voice: "Do not be afraid" (v. 10).

Maybe their empty-handedness, their openness, enables them to truly see and hear the good news of the gospel. They have arrived at the tomb with no preconceived ideas of what they will do, no obligations or expectations. They come to see—to bear witness, to simply be with Jesus and to be with each other.

Sometimes what we expect to see keeps us from seeing what is really there. Too often we do whatever it is we are equipped and prepared to do, even if it turns out that our planned work is not particularly needed. So I think we have much to learn from Mary Magdalene and "the other Mary." Because it's hard to show up empty-handed. To simply arrive at a place of tragedy carrying our grief and nothing else. I'd much rather have spices in hand. I'd much rather have phone calls to make or a service to plan. It seems so helpless, so pointless, to just go and *see*. But what might happen if we did that more often? What visions might we witness? What unexpected life might we encounter?

The women in Matthew's version share the intense and mixed emotions of the women in Mark. While "terror and amazement" seize the women in Mark (16:8), the Marys in Matthew leave the tomb "with fear and great joy" (28:8). That first Easter morning seems to have been much more complicated and nuanced than our contemporary Easter celebrations might suggest. Joy is what we like to focus on, and there is nothing wrong with joy. Joy is a good and holy thing to strive for, to highlight, to receive in the Easter season and all year long. Joy is certainly part of the story.

But the joy of Easter is mixed with terror and fear. Because resurrection life is a daunting proposition. It takes courage to accept life in its fullness—for others and for ourselves. If Jesus had stayed dead, the women would have known what to do. They knew how to grieve. But what are they supposed to do with resurrection? It threatens their entire understanding of the world. It pushes them out—way out—of their comfort zone.

Life expects far more of us than death ever will.

And in Matthew, just maybe, Mary Magdalene and the other Mary have a sense of this, because they do not bring the spices needed to anoint a dead body. They bring themselves and their curiosity. They are, I believe, ready to be amazed; ready to go, despite their fear; ready to share out of their joy.

CONNECT

Follow the example of the two Marys: Go someplace empty-handed and simply observe whatever and whoever is around you.

CONSIDER

In this Easter season, what do you need to set down so your spirit can be open to receive the good news you might encounter in the coming days?

THURSDAY
MARY MAGDALENE IN JOHN

READ

John 20:1–10

REFLECT

In many contexts, darkness is good—it can represent holy mystery, comfort and safety, cool rest and quiet. The writer of John's gospel, however, rather heavy-handedly uses "darkness" and "night" to signify things that are not of God. This starts in the first chapter of John, where the "light shines in the darkness" (1:5) and continues on into Jesus' words at the Last Supper, where he refers to himself as the "light" over and against "the darkness" (8:12; 12:35, 46). So when we read that Mary Magdalene came to the tomb "while it was still dark" (20:1), we should recognize immediately that, in John, this description does more than just alert us to the time of day. The fact that "it was still dark" suggests that those who love Jesus are still experiencing his absence deeply; they are still in the wilderness of their grief. A general aura of gloom and hopelessness envelops Jesus' friends and followers in the aftermath of his violent death.

It is still dark. We know that feeling. When something terrible happens, like the death of a loved one, there is an initial jolt of pain and horror and grief. It can be completely overwhelming. As Mary Magdalene stood near the cross, watching Jesus die; as she followed Joseph of Arimathea and watched him lay Jesus' body in the tomb; as she watched the stone cover the tomb entrance, the pain must have been acute. How can we even stand to watch our loved ones suffer? How can we bear the reality that they are dead? The immediacy of Jesus' death likely felt unbearable.

And then it is Sabbath. Mary has a chance to rest, to breathe, to let her mind and her body process all that has happened. By the time Sabbath is over she is, at least, functional again. But it is still dark. Mary still carries much uncertainty and grief as she comes to the tomb. And through this darkness she sees that the stone has been rolled away from the entrance. While the women in the other gospels go—or at least look—into the tomb, here Mary immediately runs to tell two other disciples about what has happened.

Except, of course, she doesn't know what has happened. And what she tells Simon Peter and the other disciple is not true: "They have taken the Lord out of the tomb" (v. 2). She's not lying on purpose, of course. It's just that it's still dark. She can't see clearly, and so she assumes the worst. She assumes the only explanation she can imagine: Jesus' dead body has been stolen. Nothing else makes sense. How could the one she saw killed be alive? How could an angel have moved the stone? How could God be this present and powerful? It must be that someone stole the body. That really and truly is the only logical explanation. And it's also a false explanation.

I wonder how often we fail to perceive divine power and presence because we simply cannot imagine the astonishing truth. I wonder how often we inadvertently tell stories—to ourselves and others—that present the only logical explanation, not realizing that the *real* explanation is not logical at all.

In Mary's case we can understand why resurrection is not what she immediately thinks of when she discovers that Jesus' body is missing. The dead returning to life is, after all, technically impossible. But why, I wonder, do we so often jump to the worst-case (or at least a bad-case) scenario when we encounter something unexpected? When a loved one doesn't answer a text right away, I think maybe they were in an accident. When someone declines an invitation, it must be because they are mad at me. If I wake up with a scratchy throat, it's probably COVID or cancer.

Of course, in all these situations, something bad may have happened. And if it has, we are better off facing it than living in denial. But maybe Mary Magdalene can inspire us to open our minds a bit and not jump to negative conclusions too quickly. And maybe, when we do find ourselves in a "dark" place, she can inspire us to do what she does and go tell other people. Other people who will look for themselves. When we enter a situation that seems terrible, there is value in returning to that place with friends when the sun is just a little higher in the sky, when the darkness has lifted a bit and we can, perhaps, perceive more clearly.

CONNECT

In the wilderness, it can help to seek community. Talk with a friend about a difficult, frightening, or confusing situation in your life.

CONSIDER

Think about a time when you assumed a situation to be worse than it actually was. Why do you think you made that assumption? How did you come to a clearer understanding? How might you avoid making negative assumptions in the future?

FRIDAY
MARY MAGDALENE BEARS WITNESS

READ

John 20:11–18

REFLECT

The angels ask Mary, "Woman, why are you weeping?" (v. 13).

It's difficult to read tone on a page, especially across two thousand years. Is this a sincere question? A gentle query because they really do not know why Mary is weeping? Maybe they are confused by her tears because they assume she knows about the resurrection. From their heavenly perspective, perhaps such things are obvious. Maybe human grief in general is perplexing to them. They are concerned, they are curious, and so they ask, Why are you weeping?

Or maybe these words carry an edge. The angels might be frustrated that these dense humans can't see what is (or, in this case, is not) right in front of them. "Woman, why are you crying? Jesus isn't even dead! Get over yourself."

Whatever their tone, Mary answers with what she thinks is the truth: "They have taken away my Lord, and I don't know where they have laid him" (v. 13). I imagine the angels are confused by her words, but they don't have any time to respond before Jesus himself shows up and asks Mary the same question: "Why are you weeping?" Then Jesus adds another: "Whom are you looking for?" (v. 15).

On the surface, the answers are obvious. She is weeping because Jesus was killed. She is looking for Jesus—or at least his body. But Jesus already knows these answers. Perhaps he is asking something less obvious. What exactly is it that Mary feels she has lost with his death? What is the root of her grief? Why did she love him, and what is she missing? Who does she think Jesus is? Is she really looking for Jesus, or is she searching for a messiah figure she created and projected onto him?

So often when we are sad, our grief isn't really about the thing that triggers the tears. There can be layers of grief, a complex mix of feelings that might be only tangentially related to the immediate situation. This question is not as simple as it might first appear: Why are you crying?

And so often we don't really know what we are looking for. We might think we know, but then when we find it, we decide we actually want something else. Or we realize that what we were looking for merely *represented* our longings but wasn't actually the thing itself. It is a question we should not answer too quickly: Whom (or what) are you looking for?

These questions from the angels and Jesus to Mary are not as easy as they first appear. Mary would do well to spend some time with them, to consider them carefully. But instead she answers quickly, because she is caught up in the story she created and the anxiety she feels based on that story: Jesus' body has been taken away! Rather than carefully consider the questions, she repeats the story her anxiety has produced: Jesus' body has been stolen.

It only takes one word from Jesus to cut through her anxiety and bring her clearly into the present. One word that makes her realize whom she is talking to, that shows her the fallacy of the story she's been telling. When Jesus speaks her name, Mary suddenly realizes that the One she is looking for is, in fact, standing right in front of her.

At Jesus' urging, Mary goes once again to the other disciples and tells them what she has seen. The first time she went she told the story she *thought* was true. Now she goes and tells the story that *is* true, the story that Jesus shared with her, the story of resurrection life.

Somehow, Mary's earlier story of a missing dead body prompted Simon Peter and the other disciple to run to the tomb, but this pronouncement of the gospel, of the truth of the resurrection, seems to spur no footrace or even a leisurely stroll to check out the tomb situation. The disciples stay where they are, and Jesus comes to them later that evening.

Mary Magdalene is the messenger, the traveler. She goes back and forth between Jesus and the rest of the disciples. She moves from her logical story to the fantastical truth. She moves from grief to joy, from weeping to proclaiming. She is, as many have pointed out, the first witness to the resurrection, the apostle to the apostles. She is the one called by name and sent into the wilderness as bearer of life and good news.

CONNECT

This coming weekend, listen to a woman preach. (There are many sermons and worship services available online if a woman is not preaching at your church this weekend.)

CONSIDER

When did you last weep? What was the instigating reason for your tears? Were there reasons underneath the reason?

SATURDAY
THE WOMAN FLEES TO THE WILDERNESS

READ

Revelation 12:1–6, 13–16

REFLECT

It seems fitting to end this devotional in the book of Revelation. Not only because it is the last book in the Bible, but also because Revelation is its own kind of wilderness. It is strange and unfamiliar, it is a little bit frightening, and it is an easy place in which to get lost. Revelation is an apocalyptic text, which means that it is not to be taken literally, but rather to be read at the level of symbolism and allegory, the depths of which we cannot delve into here.

According to dominant understandings of this passage, "the woman" in Revelation 12 symbolizes either Mary the mother of Jesus or the church—or both. While I don't have the scholarly expertise to stake a claim about *who* or *what* the woman represents, given the symbolic nature of apocalyptic literature, I'm sure she represents something. She is not literally a woman wearing the sun and using the moon as a footrest. Still, I'm intrigued to think about this woman as a biblical *character*. I believe her flight to the wilderness has something to teach us as we come to the end of our journey with biblical women in the wilderness.

We began our journey with Eve, the powerful mother of humanity, and we end with "the woman," who is another powerful mother figure. When we meet "the woman," she is clothed in light and creating life. As she prepares to give birth, a dragon waits to devour her child.

I realize that the visual image of this scene is startling and otherworldly, but the core reality of the scenario feels all too familiar. How many women today, in all their radiance and power, give birth to and care for children whom they fear the world is—in one way or another—waiting to devour?

179

Racial injustice, violence against women, hate crimes and laws that dehumanize LGBTQIA people, environmental catastrophes, and viral pandemics—there are many dragons lurking, waiting for our children.

The woman's newborn child is "snatched away" (presumably by angels?) and taken to God for protection (v. 5). But the woman must get to her protected space of her own volition. She flees to the wilderness, "where she has a place prepared by God" (v. 6). Isn't that a lovely thought, that God has created a place of safety and nurture for us in the wilderness? Just like Hagar, this woman flees to the wilderness for protection. In the wilderness, both Hagar and the woman of Revelation encounter and dwell with God. This powerful and mysterious woman of Revelation is nourished by God in the wilderness for 1,260 days.

After the angels defeat the dragon and throw him back down to earth, he once again pursues the woman; and once again she flees to the wilderness for safety. This time she is aided in her escape by being given the wings of an eagle. In a sense, it is an animal that saves her from the dragon this second time. And when the dragon tries to destroy her by flood, the earth itself comes to her rescue and swallows up the water.

There are dangers in the wilderness, to be sure. But there is also nurture and protection. While the wilderness is often unsettling and unpredictable, it can also be a space away from the threats of the world, a place to rest, regroup, and receive.

So many things are true all at once. We are people of power and light. And there are dragons waiting to devour the goodness we labor to bring into the world. We can flee to protect ourselves. And we need the strength of other creatures and of the earth itself to ensure our survival. The wilderness is a place of disorientation and scarcity—and also of safety and nurture. In the wilds of the wilderness, may you find those places that God has prepared for you; may you receive the nourishment that God offers in the most unlikely landscapes.

CONNECT

What is a wild place that you love? Spend some time there.

CONSIDER

What would it mean for God to have prepared a place in the wilderness for you? What might that place be? What kind of nourishment would you receive? How long do you need to stay? How often can you return?

Blessing for the Second Sunday of Easter: From the Women Who Proclaim Jesus' Resurrection

Fear and boldness,
astonishment and joy—
we have a story to tell.
You think you know this story,
but listen anyway.
Because we thought we knew what was in the tomb,
but we looked anyway.
So even though we all think we understand how the world works,
let's be curious anyway.

Whether you come with a task
or show up empty-handed;
whether you have a clear plan
or just hope for the best;
whether you arrive in the dimness of predawn
or the bright light of day;
unimaginable Life awaits;
the unbelievable miracle of Resurrection has already happened.

You don't have to imagine it—though there is joy in imagining.
You don't have to believe it—though there is peace in believing.

You just have to wander in the wilderness of your life
with an open heart
a faithful spirit
a committed presence.

In the end, you will find your way.
And as you journey, we offer this blessing:
　　May you be amazed and astonished
　　by the resurrection life of God within, among, and around you.
Amen.

Guides for Group Use

WORSHIP GUIDE

Just as the Israelites wandered the wilderness together, we also journey through this season of Lent as faith communities. This guide is designed to support congregations that would like to engage the stories of these wilderness women in the context of worship. While these worship liturgies connect to the material in the devotion reflections, they will prove meaningful even for those who are not using the book for their daily reading.

This guide includes liturgies that can be used any or every week and specific worship pieces for each Sunday. There are also worship suggestions for Ash Wednesday, Maundy Thursday, and Good Friday. I hope that this material can offer support to those planning worship for their communities in this sacred season.

DIGITAL DOWNLOAD

A digital download is available from Herald Press and includes the following resources:

- Digital files of the images from this book created by Michelle Burkholder

- Sunday blessings from each week

- Liturgies from this worship guide

Purchase of this resource grants the purchaser permission to display and make copies of the images and texts for use in personal and ministry settings. (To purchase, go to qrco.de/prone-to-wander.)

WORSHIP IMAGES

Pastor and artist Michelle Burkholder has created beautiful images to accompany the blessings in this book. Within communities that purchase the digital download, these images can be used in worship in a variety of ways, including as bulletin cover art, as coloring pages for children (and adults), on banners in the worship space, or as projected images for reflection and meditation.

OFFERTORY PRAYER

(to be used any or every week)

God of provision, God of abundance,
we have gathered what gifts we could here in the wilderness.
In the midst of uncertainty, it is tempting to hold as much as we can;
to keep all for ourselves because we do not know
      where our wandering will lead
    or how long it might last.
So we give this offering in fear and in faith,
trusting that there is enough for us all.
Honor our fear. Honor our faith. Honor our trust.
Honor these gifts, O God, and use them for your love.
Amen.

SERMON SUGGESTIONS

The corresponding daily reflections are listed with the suggested scripture readings for each Sunday in this worship guide. These reflections provide insight into the texts and ideas for preaching. The "Consider" sections after each indicated reflection might also suggest useful illustrations and modern-day connections helpful for preaching.

ALTERNATIVE BLESSING

(*to be used any or every week in place of the blessings suggested in the weekly liturgies*)

On this Lenten journey,
    may your wandering heart find its true home
    in the One who walks with you through the wilderness. Amen.

LENTEN COMMUNION LITURGY

(*suitable for any Sunday in Lent when you share the Lord's Supper*)

Invitation to the Table

God prepares a table for us in the wilderness:
Abundant bread in the midst of scarcity,
overflowing cups in a parched land,
friends to travel with us on the journey,
a pillar of fire by night to show the way.

Come, my friends, and let us share this meal.
Let us rest from our wandering;
let us receive divine grace;
let us remember together:
"That the Lord Jesus on the night when he was betrayed took a loaf of
    bread,
and when he had given thanks, he broke it and said,
'This is my body that is for you. Do this in remembrance of me.'
In the same way he took the cup also, after supper, saying,
'This cup is the new covenant in my blood. Do this, as often as you drink
    it, in remembrance of me.'

For as often as [we] eat this bread and drink the cup,
[we] proclaim the Lord's death until he comes" (1 Corinthians
11:23b–26).

Prayer of Thanksgiving

God of the wilderness,
we give you thanks for the nourishment you provide to our wandering
spirits.
For the bread of life in the midst of death,
for the cup of joy in the midst of grief,
for each person gathered to share this sacred meal,
we give you thanks.

ASH WEDNESDAY
FOUNT OF EVERY BLESSING

In addition to the imposition of ashes, this Ash Wednesday service offers an opportunity for people to consider spiritual practices and commitments for the season of Lent. If the congregation is using *Prone to Wander* as a community, you might offer a general introduction to the book and discuss ways that people can use the material throughout the season. If the full group is not using this book, you could instead invite people into a more general conversation about Lenten spiritual practices.

SCRIPTURE READINGS

Psalm 139:1–18
Genesis 3:19–24 (Saturday after Ash Wednesday)

HYMN

"Come, Thou Fount"

PRAYER

Holy One, our fount of every blessing,
as we enter the wilderness of Lent,
let our ears be tuned to hear your voice,
let our eyes be tuned to see your face,
let our hearts be tuned to sing your grace.

Though we are prone to wander, you continue seeking us;
though we face danger, you have come to rescue us;
though this wilderness landscape changes, your love remains constant.

We offer our hearts to your tender mercy.
By your grace, bind us to you.
By your grace, may our wandering lead us safely home.
Amen.

BENEDICTION

As you wander in the wilderness, may you:
  breathe in the beauty,
  love the questions—and be brave in the asking and answering.
  May you not be ashamed;
  and may you trust that God's presence is grace.
Always grace.
Amen.

FIRST SUNDAY OF LENT
STREAMS OF MERCY

SCRIPTURE READING

Genesis 16:1–16 (Week 2: Monday and Tuesday)

CALL TO WORSHIP

Leader: Welcome, all wandering hearts.

*All: We come greeting friends and meeting strangers,
wearing our joy and bearing our grief,
sighing our questions and trying our faith.*

Leader: Welcome to the wilderness of Lent—

*All: where pretense is laid down;
where grace abounds;
where home is found.*

Leader: Welcome, all wandering hearts, to worship.

PRAYER OF CONFESSION

Leader: For the violence we enact and the violence we allow,

Congregation: God have mercy.

Leader: For the ways we limit the freedom of others,

Congregation: God have mercy.

Leader: For our failure to fully live out the freedom you give us,

Congregation: God have mercy.

Leader: In the moments we run away,

Congregation: God have mercy.

Leader: In the moments we settle in,

Congregation: God have mercy.

Leader: When we cannot bear to watch others suffer,

Congregation: God have mercy.

Leader: And in your mercy, God, let us find our home in you,

All: wherever we may wander.

191

WORDS OF ASSURANCE

Wherever you wander,
know that God makes a way in the wilderness.
The Holy One guides us, feeds us, and forgives us. Amen.

BENEDICTION

In the wilderness of the coming week:
May your wells be full.
May your life be free.
May your love be fierce.

SECOND SUNDAY OF LENT
BY THY HELP

SCRIPTURE READING

Exodus 1:22–2:10 (Acts 7:17–22) (Week 3: Tuesday and Wednesday)

CALL TO WORSHIP

Leader: In the wilderness we gather
Congregation: with friends and strangers,
All: forming a community of support.
Leader: In the wilderness we struggle
Congregation: against forces of violence,
All: conspiring together for life.
Leader: In the wilderness we wander
Congregation: through unfamiliar landscapes,
All: seeking a faithful path.
Leader: In the wilderness we worship
Congregation: our God of love and life,
All: opening ourselves to the power of the Spirit.

PRAYER OF CONFESSION

Leader: God of the wilderness,
we do not wander alone.
We honor those who have gone before
and accept responsibility for those who come behind.
We give you thanks for those who walk alongside,
our companions on the journey.
For those times we have dismissed the wisdom shared by
others,

Congregation: forgive us, O God.

Leader: For those times we have failed to consider how our
actions will affect others,

Congregation: forgive us, O God.

Leader: For those times we elevate ourselves and our preferences
above others,

Congregation: forgive us, O God.

Leader: For those times we diminish ourselves and ignore our
own needs,

Congregation: forgive us, O God.

Leader: Continue to form us into a true community,
people of faith finding our way through the wilderness
together.
Amen.

WORDS OF ASSURANCE

Wherever you wander,
know that God makes a way in the wilderness.
The Holy One guides us, feeds us, and forgives us. Amen.

BENEDICTION

When you face the forces of death,
may you meet their caution with courage,
their shortsightedness with broad perspective,
their ignorance with wisdom,
their fear with generosity,
their solemnity with celebration,
their insistence on scarcity
with songs of God's miraculous abundance.

THIRD SUNDAY OF LENT
FLAMING TONGUES

SCRIPTURE READING

Numbers 27:1–11 (Week 4: Monday)

CALL TO WORSHIP

Leader: We come to listen
Congregation: so that we can go out and speak.
Leader: We praise God's power
Congregation: so that we might rightly use our own.
Leader: We pause and pray
Congregation: so that we might plan faithfully.
Leader: We consider the ancient Scriptures
Congregation: so that we might better understand our present reality.
Leader: We continue this wilderness journey
All: following God's way together.

PRAYER OF CONFESSION

Leader: Gentle God of power, mighty God of peace,
forgive us when we fail to acknowledge the power we hold.

**Congregation: Hold us when we are powerless to protect ourselves
and those we love.**

Leader: Forgive us when fear keeps us from speaking up.

Congregation: Speak through us when we dare to open our mouths.

Leader: Forgive us when we ignore injustice.

Congregation: Work through us to create more just communities.

Leader: Forgive the violence we confuse with true power,

Congregation: and empower us to live out the power of your peace.

WORDS OF ASSURANCE

Wherever you wander,
know that God makes a way in the wilderness.
The Holy One guides us, feeds us, and forgives us. Amen.

BENEDICTION

Walk through the wilderness as your full self
without diminishment
without apology
without fear.

May God's power hold and guide you
through your strength and your weakness
in all the wilderness places.

FOURTH SUNDAY OF LENT
TUNE MY HEART

SCRIPTURE READING

1 Kings 17:8–24 (Week 5: Tuesday and Wednesday)

CALL TO WORSHIP

Leader: You are welcome in this space with all of who you are:
your body, with its pain and its pleasure;
your heart, with its passion and its longing;
your feelings of relief and grief, anger and elation.

Congregation: **We bring into this space all of who we are:**
committing to love ourselves,
endeavoring to love each other,
trusting in the fierce and eternal love of God.

All: *We offer our full selves in this time of worship.*

PRAYER OF CONFESSION

Leader: Holy God,
when our compassion is limited by fear and struggle,

Congregation: **calm our fears and ease the way.**

Leader: When our imaginations cannot extend beyond
immediate needs,

Congregation: **expand our vision and offer provision.**

Leader: When our anger flares in grief and exhaustion,

Congregation: **meet us with gentleness and comfort.**

Leader: When we hold tightly to what you want us to release,

Congregation: **grant us the grace to loosen our grasp.**

Leader: In your love, forgive us.

Congregation: **In your love, lead the way.**

WORDS OF ASSURANCE

Wherever you wander,
know that God makes a way in the wilderness.
The Holy One guides us, feeds us, and forgives us. Amen.

BENEDICTION

Walk boldly, dear ones,
through this barren landscape—
this beautiful and beckoning wilderness.
May you find a new home as you leave an old.
May you find gratitude for deep love in the strength of your grief.
May you find pleasure in all the senses of your body.
May you find your life as you lose it.
May you find each other.
And, together, may we find the way.

FIFTH SUNDAY OF LENT
WHEN A STRANGER

SCRIPTURE READING

Mark 5:21–34 (Week 6: Thursday)

CALL TO WORSHIP

Leader: We come in search of healing for ourselves and for those we love.

Congregation: We come in hope and in faith, reaching out to Jesus.

Leader: Let this be a place where our names are known and our stories honored.

Congregation: **Let this be a time when our suffering is met with compassion.**

Leader: Let this be a space for us to experience wholeness and peace.

All: *Let this be a moment when our fingertips graze the hem of the holy.*

PRAYER OF CONFESSION

Leader: Holy God,
when we would turn others away from your healing presence,

Congregation: **forgive us.**

Leader: When we are so distracted by what might be coming that we neglect what is happening in the moment,

Congregation: **show us a better way.**

Leader: When we believe we are more important than others in need,

Congregation: **forgive us.**

Leader: When we believe we are less worthy of healing than those around us,

Congregation: **call us by name.**

Leader: As we walk together in the wilderness:

All: *grant us your healing, grant us your peace.*

WORDS OF ASSURANCE

Wherever you wander,
know that God makes a way in the wilderness.
The Holy One guides us, feeds us, and forgives us. Amen.

BENEDICTION

In the wilderness, remember that
your need is not burden;
your presence is not imposition;
your body is not shameful;
your voice is not too loud.

For the sake of healing—your own and the world's—
you are allowed to interrupt and insist,
to challenge and question,
to give and receive with generosity and grace.
In the wildness of the wilderness,
may conflict and companionship
draw you ever more deeply into faith.

PALM/PASSION SUNDAY
HIS PRECIOUS BLOOD

SCRIPTURE READINGS

Luke 19:28–40 (Palm Sunday)
Luke 23:44–56 (Passion Sunday) (Holy Week: Holy Saturday)

CALL TO WORSHIP

Leader: Shout hosanna!
Congregation: Jesus comes in the name of God.
Leader: Sing songs of praise!
Congregation: Glory in the highest heaven.
Leader: We enter into this Holy Week together
Congregation: with joy and gratitude; in fear and trembling.

Leader: Let us hear the story—
Congregation: the whole story.
Leader: Let us worship in faith,
Congregation: confident of God's loving presence.

PRAYER OF CONFESSION

Leader: God of the triumphal entry,
God of the cross,
it is hard to look past the cheerful facade
and tend to the tension.
It is hard to stay in the presence of pain
when the crowds head home for lunch.
This wilderness of joy and grief, of community and conflict,
is hard to navigate.
All: ***Forgive our missteps.***
Guide our feet.

WORDS OF ASSURANCE

Wherever you wander,
know that God makes a way in the wilderness.
The Holy One guides us, feeds us, and forgives us. Amen.

BENEDICTION

I invite you to live within the fullness of this Holy Week:
from today's loud hosannas
to Friday's wailing
to Saturday's silence.
Walk slowly.
Breathe deeply.
Receive the difficult blessing of the cross.

MAUNDY THURSDAY

This worship outline includes both communion and footwashing. Feel free to adapt it to include only one or the other if that works better for your group. If you will not have a Good Friday worship service, you may wish to include elements from that outline (p. 203–5) in this service as well.

OPENING PRAYER

Holy and almighty God who stooped to wash disciples' feet,
our wilderness wandering has brought us here
    to this night of grieving and remembering.
In our hunger, we come to your table;
in our weariness, we come to be washed;
In our loneliness, we come together
    with singing and silence,
    with scripture and prayer.
Here are our hearts, O God. Take and seal them.
In your love you meet us on this wilderness path;
in your grace you welcome us to this time of worship.
Amen.

SONG

Sing a communion hymn or song familiar to your congregation.

SCRIPTURE READING

Matthew 26:20–35, 69–75

REFLECTION

Read the reflection for Tuesday of Holy Week, or invite someone to share their own thoughts on the scripture and the significance of sharing the Lord's Supper.

COMMUNION

See "Lenten Communion Liturgy" (p. 188–89).

SONG

"Come, Thou Fount"

SCRIPTURE READING

John 12:1–8

REFLECTION

Read the reflection for Monday of Holy Week, or invite someone to share their own thoughts on this passage and its connection to Jesus' act of foot-washing during the Last Supper.

SCRIPTURE READING

John 13:1–5

FOOTWASHING

Offer the opportunity for people to have their feet or hands washed and to wash the feet or hands of another. (Provide an easy way for people to opt out of this activity.)

SONG

Sing some Taizé hymns or other songs during the footwashing time or choose a closing song familiar to your congregation.

BENEDICTION

In your hunger, may you find the bread of life.
In your weariness, may you be met with refreshing waters.
In your loneliness, may you know God's loving accompaniment
on this wandering and wonderful wilderness path.

GOOD FRIDAY

This outline is for a simple Good Friday service. Specific hymns are suggested, but there may be different songs that work better for your congregation. If you did not offer a Maundy Thursday worship service, you may wish to include elements from that outline (p. 201–2) in this service as well.

OPENING PRAYER

Holy God,
we are privileged to be your people
and to be part of your story.
We have gathered to walk through the most difficult piece of the story
together.
This is a story from ancient times,
yet it is still a familiar story today.
This world, too often, is still a Good Friday world.
Let these scriptures remind us that you walk with us through it all.
In this wilderness of injustice, lead us down your righteous path.
In this wilderness of violence, guide us to your gentleness.
In this wilderness of condemnation, show us your mercy.
In this wilderness of fear, give us your peace.
In this time of worship,
give us hearts to receive all that you will offer.
Amen.

SONG

"Come, Thou Fount"

SCRIPTURE READING

Luke 23:26–31

REFLECTION

Read the reflection for Thursday of Holy Week, or invite someone to share their own thoughts on this passage.

SONG

"Kyrie" (any version familiar to your congregation)

SCRIPTURE READING

Luke 23:32–43

SONG

"Jesus Remember Me" (Taizé)

SCRIPTURE READING

Luke 23:44–56

REFLECTION

Read the reflection for Saturday of Holy Week, or invite someone to share their own thoughts on this passage.

SONG

"Were You There?"

CLOSING

Reflect further on the story of Jesus' crucifixion, or invite people into an attitude of contemplation and rest for the remaining hours of Good Friday and into Holy Saturday.

BENEDICTION

In this wilderness of injustice, may you follow the righteous path.

In this wilderness of violence, may you be guided in God's gentleness.

In this wilderness of condemnation, may you know Christ's mercy.

In this wilderness of fear, may you have the Spirit's peace.

May your broken-open heart receive all that the Holy One longs to give.

EASTER SUNDAY
SONGS OF LOUDEST PRAISE

SCRIPTURE READING

Luke 24:1–12 (Tuesday of Easter Season)

CALL TO WORSHIP

Leader: On the first day of the week, at early dawn, the women went to the tomb.

Congregation: **On this first day of the week, a little past early dawn, we have come to worship.**

Leader: The women took the spices they had prepared.

Congregation: **We bring ourselves, prepared, like the women, to find what we expect.**

Leader: But what if we find the unexpected? The unimaginable? The unbelievable?

Congregation: **What if we find the stone rolled away? The tomb empty? The dazzling presence?**

Leader: What if we find life where we expect death? Good news where we expect grief?

Congregation: **Are we prepared for that? Are we prepared for Easter?**

All: *Let us worship this morning in holy expectation.*

PRAYER OF CONFESSION

Leader: God of Life,
too often we look for the living among the dead,

Congregation: unable to imagine the fullness of your presence.

Leader: Too often we respond to good news with fear,

Congregation: not understanding what resurrection life really means.

Leader: Too often we fail to remember

Congregation: who you are and what you have promised.

Leader: When our imaginations fail,
when our faith falters,

All: forgive us, O God.

WORDS OF ASSURANCE

Through the power of the resurrection, God makes a way in the
wilderness.

The Holy One guides us, feeds us, and forgives us. Amen.

BENEDICTION

On this Resurrection Sunday,

in this Easter season,

may your wilderness be renewed.

May you find stones rolled away.

May light flood the shadowy places.

May you hear good news where you least expect it.

And if you don't—can't—understand it all,

may you receive it anyway:

All the openness, all the joy, all the life.

EASTER SEASON WORSHIP

If you would like to continue the theme of women in the wilderness into the Easter season, you could spend one Sunday on each of the gospel accounts of the resurrection with a focus on the women who go to the tomb. The reflections for the week after Easter Sunday will be helpful in such a series. Worship elements in this outline can be used with any of the gospel readings throughout the season.

CALL TO WORSHIP

Leader: Hallelujah!
Congregation: Hallelujah!
Leader: We have come to worship our God of life, whose power raised Jesus from the tomb,
Congregation: whose power raises us to new vision, new joy, new love.
Leader: Hallelujah!
Congregation: Hallelujah!
All: Let us worship in spirit and truth.

BENEDICTION

May you be amazed and astonished
by the resurrection life of God within, among, and around you.

SMALL GROUP /
SUNDAY SCHOOL GUIDE

This is a suggested outline for small groups or Sunday school classes. The opening prayer and blessing provided here can be used every week to open and close the sessions. Specific suggestions for *centering, listening,* and *discussing* are provided for each weekly session. Feel free to adapt this material as needed to fit the practice of your group.

OPENING PRAYER

Depending on the preferences of the group, you may wish to begin each session with a time of sharing joys and concerns followed by an extemporaneous prayer for what has been shared. The prayer below is suitable for those who prefer to use a prewritten prayer.

Holy One, fount of all our blessings,
we thank you for each person gathered here and for this time that we
have together.
We thank you for the ways you speak to us
through Scripture and silence,
through conversation and contemplation.
Tune our hearts to receive your word.
Let us know your presence with us in our wilderness wandering.
Amen.

CENTERING

The centering activity is designed to help people focus on their presence together and God's presence with them as they prepare to read and discuss Scripture. While a different centering activity is suggested for each week, you may choose to repeat one or two of the activities that seem to work well for your group.

LISTENING

The suggested scripture readings are substantial. Give some thought to how people will hear the text each week. You might invite one person to prepare the reading, have multiple people read a few verses each, or even share a video presentation of the passage.

DISCUSSING

The group discussion is the heart of these gatherings. Various "Consider" questions from the daily reflections are suggested for each session to help people make connections between the scripture and their lives. People will be able to discuss these questions regardless of whether they have read the reflections in this book. And if the conversation wanders away from the given prompts, just enjoy seeing where the Holy Spirit will take you!

BLESSING

May you receive manna in the wilderness.
May you find streams in the desert.
May you know that God's grace accompanies and holds you
in all your wilderness wandering.

FIRST SUNDAY OF LENT (OR WEEK AFTER)
STREAMS OF MERCY ~ HAGAR

CENTERING

Invite people to turn to the labyrinth image in their books (p. 12). (If not everyone in the group has a book, you can purchase the digital download from Herald Press, which grants permission for you to print as many copies of the labyrinth as desired. For more information, visit qrco.de/prone-to-wander.) As people trace the path from the entrance to the center of the labyrinth, encourage them to silently offer to God whatever they are carrying—joys, struggles, pain, fear, worries, or anything else on their minds. As people reach the center, take a few moments to breathe deeply. As people trace the path out, invite them to be aware of God's presence and to receive whatever God is offering them in response to what they have offered to God.

LISTENING

Read Genesis 21:8–21.

DISCUSSING

Use the "Consider" questions for Wednesday, Thursday, and Friday of week 2 (pp. 46–52).

SECOND SUNDAY OF LENT (OR WEEK AFTER)
BY THY HELP ~ MIRIAM

CENTERING

Sing one or more songs that are familiar and beloved by your community. If nobody is available to lead such singing, you could play a recording or video of a song and invite people to sing along or simply listen.

LISTENING

Read Exodus 14:21–30; 15:20–21; Numbers 12:1–16.

DISCUSSING

Use the "Consider" questions for Friday or Saturday of week 3 (pp. 74–77). If the group wishes to focus the discussion more on the aspect of celebration (Exodus reading), you can have a conversation about heart songs and perhaps even do some planning for an upcoming Easter (or other) celebration. A focus on issues of power (Numbers reading) could lead to discussions about power dynamics in group members' families, your congregation, or the broader community.

THIRD SUNDAY OF LENT (OR WEEK AFTER)
FLAMING TONGUES ~ VASHTI

CENTERING

Introduce the practice of *statio* (Latin for "position" or "location"). This can be used to open group gatherings, and people can also use it on their own as a way to pause and move throughout the day. Statio marks a transition into a new activity or state of being with a focus on God's presence.

Invite people to settle their bodies into a comfortable position. Ring a chime or bell to indicate the beginning of statio. During this time, ask people to either close their eyes or find a focal point and breathe deeply and intentionally. After 1–3 minutes, ring the bell or chime three times to indicate an end of statio.

LISTENING

Read Esther 1:5–22.

DISCUSSING

Use the "Consider" questions from Tuesday, Thursday, and Friday of week 4 (pp. 87–96) to guide a discussion about how we view and use power.

FOURTH SUNDAY OF LENT (OR WEEK AFTER)
TUNE MY HEART ~ THE BELOVED (FROM SONG OF SONGS)

CENTERING

Have paper and colored pencils, pens, or markers available. Ask people to write the word *love* in the middle of their papers. Then invite them to write the names of people they love and who love them all around the page. Invite them to pray for these people as they draw circles around the names and connect them to the word *love* in the center.

LISTENING

Read Song of Songs 2:1–17; 8:1–7.

DISCUSSING

Use the "Consider" questions from Thursday and Friday of week 5 (pp. 115–18). You might also discuss this question: How does our experience of human love affect our understanding of God's love?

FIFTH SUNDAY OF LENT (OR THE WEEK AFTER)
WHEN A STRANGER ~ THE WOMAN AT THE WELL

CENTERING

Invite people to engage in the "Connect" suggestion from Tuesday of week 6 (p. 131): Close your eyes, take a few deep breaths, and imagine yourself talking to Jesus. What questions do you have for him? What might his answers be?

LISTENING

Read John 4.

DISCUSSING

Use the "Consider" questions from Monday and Tuesday of week 6 (pp. 128–31). You might also discuss these questions:

- Is there anything you would like to share from today's centering activity?

- What do you think Jesus means by "living water"?

- Tell about a time you felt that you received living water from God.

PALM/PASSION SUNDAY (OR HOLY WEEK)
HIS PRECIOUS BLOOD ~ MARY OF BETHANY

CENTERING

Share together in footwashing, handwashing, or anointing, depending on the comfort level of your group and what is generally practiced in your tradition. For this Holy Week gathering, the centering ritual might take more time than the discussion portion.

LISTENING

Read John 12:1–8.

DISCUSSING

Use the "Consider" questions from Holy Monday and Maundy Thursday (pp. 149, 155). The "Connect" prompt for Maundy Thursday might also be helpful.

RETREAT GUIDE

As Lent is a season for heightened spiritual reflection, it can be a good time to set aside a few days for retreat. The first outline is a suggested schedule outline for a group retreat, which could be held any weekend during Lent. The second outline includes suggestions for a personal at-home retreat to engage over the Easter Triduum—from Maundy Thursday evening through Easter Sunday evening.

GROUP LENTEN RETREAT

The outline suggests two options for content. The *general overview* option coordinates with suggestions given in the "Worship Guide" (pp. 186–207). The *week intensive* option goes through each session for one particular week—perhaps the week in which you are holding the retreat.

FRIDAY EVENING

Share supper together

Opening Worship

General overview *and* week intensive options: Welcome to the Wilderness: Exodus 13:17–22 (Ash Wednesday)

Suggested order of worship:

- Welcome, retreat overview, announcements
- Song or music
- Prayer
- Scripture reading
- Reflection: Read the Ash Wednesday reflection or invite someone to speak briefly on the scripture

- Song or songs
- Benediction (see the "Worship Guide" for a benediction suggestion, p. 190)

Small Group Session 1

General overview option: Genesis 16:1–16 (Week 2: Monday and Tuesday)

Week intensive option: Monday of chosen week

Suggested outline for small group sessions:
- Invite individuals to introduce themselves (if everyone does not already know each other) and answer a brief get-to-know-you question. The question could be something standard about family, jobs, pets, favorite foods, hobbies, and so on, or something more unexpected, like "If you were a vegetable, what kind would you be and why?"

- Listen to the chosen scripture passage. You can choose one reader or go around the group having each person read a verse at a time.

- Discuss the "Consider" questions from the designated reflection or reflections along with any other thoughts that emerge from listening to the text.

- End in prayer.

SATURDAY

Breakfast

Large Group Session 1

General overview option: Exodus 1:22–2:10; Acts 7:17–22 (Week 3: Tuesday and Wednesday)

Week intensive option: Tuesday of chosen week

Suggested outline for large group sessions:

- Gather the group together by offering a prayer and sharing any announcements about what is coming up during the retreat.

- Sing one or more songs.

- Have someone read the designated scripture passage.

- Allow for 1–5 minutes of silence for people to consider the passage.

- Have someone read the designated reflection.

- Engage the "Connect" activities or "Consider" questions from the daily reflection or reflections as seems helpful for your group.

Small Group Session 2

General overview option: Numbers 27:1–11 (Week 4: Monday)

Week intensive option: Wednesday of chosen week

See Small Group Session 1 for outline.

Personal time

Allow participants to spend some time on their own. People might want to journal, pray, walk, rest, read, draw, or engage in other activities that will help them process the retreat material.

Lunch

Small Group Session 3

General overview option: 1 Kings 17:8–24 (Week 5: Tuesday and Wednesday)

Week intensive option: Thursday of chosen week

See Small Group Session 1 for outline.

Personal time

See personal time information earlier in the day.

Large Group Session 2

General overview option: Mark 5:21–34 (Week 6: Thursday)

Week intensive option: Friday of chosen week; end with blessing from Sunday of chosen week

See Large Group Session 1 for outline.

Supper

Personal time or group activity

See personal time information earlier in the day. Possible group activities in-clude watching a movie, having a campfire, or playing board games.

SUNDAY

Small Group Session 4

General overview option: Luke 23:44–56 (Holy Week: Holy Saturday)

Week intensive option: Saturday of chosen week

See Small Group Session 1 for outline.

Closing Worship

General overview *and* week intensive options: Women Bear Witness to Jesus' Death: Luke 23:44–56 (Holy Week: Holy Saturday)

See the Opening Worship section for suggested order of worship, or follow your congregation's traditional order for Sunday morning worship.

End with lunch together

AT-HOME EASTER TRIDUUM RETREAT

The suggestions in this outline will allow you to maintain a spiritual focus for the holy days of Maundy Thursday through Easter, even if you are not able to get away for a full retreat.

MAUNDY THURSDAY EVENING

- If you have not already done so, read the reflection and engage in the "Connect" and "Consider" suggestions for Maundy Thursday.

- If possible, attend a Maundy Thursday service at your church or another church in your community. If no appropriate services are available, watch a video of a Maundy Thursday service online, or read John 13 with friends or family members.

GOOD FRIDAY

Morning

- Use the labyrinth on page 12 as you center yourself for this holy day.

- Read the Good Friday scripture and reflection.

- Journal about or discuss the "Consider" questions.

Midday

- Read Mark 15.

- Sit in silence for 5 minutes.

- Engage in the "Connect" activity for Good Friday.

Evening

- If possible, attend a Good Friday service at your church or another church in your community. Alternatively, watch a video of a Good Friday service online (perhaps a Good Friday Taizé service), or read John 18–19.

HOLY SATURDAY

Treat this day as a Sabbath, whatever that means for you. Consider refraining from work, social media, and commerce. Spend time doing things that nourish your body and spirit.

Morning

- Read the Holy Saturday scripture and reflection.

- Engage in the Holy Saturday "Connect" and "Consider" suggestions.

Midday

- Spend time outside appreciating God's creation.

Evening

- Spend time appreciating human creativity: look at artwork, read some poetry, or listen to music.

- Before you go to bed, use the labyrinth on page 12 as you offer your prayers to God and receive God's blessing.

EASTER SUNDAY

Morning

- Attend Easter Sunday worship.

Midday

- Spend time with family or friends.

Evening

- Read the Easter Sunday blessing and contemplate the accompanying artwork.

NOTES

1 Wilda C. Gafney, *Womanist Midrash: A Reintroduction to the Women of the Torah and the Throne* (Westminster John Knox Press, 2017), 20–22.

2 Phyllis Trible, *Texts of Terror: Literary Feminist Readings of Biblical Narratives* (Fortress Press, 1984), 18.

3 Gafney, *Womanist Midrash*, 36.

4 Gafney, *Womanist Midrash*, 99–100.

5 Emma Hinchliffe, "The Share of Fortune 500 Companies Run by Women CEOs Stays Flat at 10.4% as Pace of Change Stalls," *Fortune*, June 4, 2024, https://fortune.com/2024/06/04/fortune-500-companies-women-ceos-2024/.

6 As of this writing, there have been forty-six presidencies, but forty-five men have filled the role, as Grover Cleveland served nonconsecutive terms.

THE AUTHOR

Rev. Joanna Harader (she/her) is the author *of Expecting Emmanuel* and frequently posts words for worship on her blog, *Spacious Faith*. Her worship liturgies have been published in the *Voices Together* hymnal and are used in churches of various denominations. She has written for publications such as *Leader* magazine, Shine Sunday school curriculum, and *Christian Century*. Joanna serves as pastor of Bethel College Mennonite Church in North Newton, Kansas.

THE ARTIST

Rev. Michelle Burkholder (they/them) serves as associate pastor of Hyattsville (MD) Mennonite Church and is a practicing visual artist. Michelle's art was part of Joanna's previous book, *Expecting Emmanuel*. Another one of Michelle's paper cutout pieces, *Loaves and Fishes*, can be found in the *Voices Together* hymnal. Michelle studied art at Eastern Mennonite University and the intersections of theology and the arts at United Theological Seminary of the Twin Cities. The connections between art, faith, and spirituality fill Michelle with wonder, curiosity, and joy.